ANIMAL HEROES

ANIMAL HEROES

Yvonne Roberts

PELHAM BOOKS

Stephen Greene Press

To James and Andrew

PELHAM BOOKS/Stephen Greene Press

Published by the Penguin Group
27 Wrights Lane, London W8 5TZ, England
Viking Penguin Inc., 40 West 23rd Street, New York, New York 10010, USA
The Stephen Greene Press Inc., 15 Muzzey Street, Lexington,
Massachusetts 02173, USA
Penguin Books Australia Ltd, Ringwood, Victoria, Australia
Penguin Books Canada Ltd, 2801 John Street, Markham, Ontario,
Canada L3R 1B4
Penguin Books (NZ) Ltd, 182–190 Wairau Road, Auckland 10, New Zealand

Penguin Books Ltd, Registered Offices: Harmondsworth, Middlesex, England

First published 1990

Library of Congress No. 89–64336

ISBN 0 7207 1937 2

Made and printed in Great Britain by
Richard Clay Ltd, Bungay, Suffolk
Typeset in 10/12pt Palatino by Cambrian Typesetters, Frimley, Surrey

Contents

Acknowledgements

MY GRATEFUL THANKS to all the charities, institutions, companies, private individuals and owners who supplied me with information for this book. A special mention for their help also goes to my sister Gail and her friends for their assistance and translations, Mr & Mrs Wankling, Ann Lycett of Ullapool Library, Jane Read B. Vet. Med., MRCVS, Miss Y. Wren – photographer, Don Short, Hilary Foakes – editor and my husband James for his encouragement and support.

Foreword

THE PEOPLE'S DISPENSARY FOR SICK ANIMALS (PDSA) is pleased to be associated with this book since its own name is so inexorably linked with that of the Dickin Medal, popularly 'the animal V.C.', which was awarded during the Second World War to those animals displaying conspicuous gallantry and devotion in the course of their duties with the Civil Defence and Armed Forces. Both Society and Medal were the inspiration of Maria Dickin who was acutely aware of the importance of the relationship between animals and man. Today the Society stands, the largest specifically veterinary charity in the country, as a tribute to her perspicacity, but in their daily activities its personnel are constantly reminded of the continuing need for greater understanding and goodwill in the field of human and animal interaction. Hopefully the positive and uplifting tone of the anecdotes here related will contribute to this.

Edward Jones.

D. E. Jones BSc., BVSc., PhD., MRCVS.
Information Services Manager
The People's Dispensary for Sick Animals

Introduction

HARDLY A WEEK seems to go by without the media reporting an incident where an animal has alerted its owner to a fire or perhaps been the hero of some other drama. It was precisely these types of stories which prompted me to write this book – after all, if I enjoyed reading about them, perhaps other people did too.

As I searched for information, I became acutely aware of some of the terrible things that have happened to animals, but I decided that I would deliberately avoid such details in the book. My main aim was that this book should be enjoyable to read – a celebration of animals – rather than one which dwells on cruelty.

In one dictionary the word 'hero' is defined as 'one greatly regarded for his achievements or qualities', so in relation to animals I have included accounts such as assisting the authorities, saving lives, helping other animals, using ingenuity and displaying incredible loyalty. As my collection of stories grew, I was amazed at the unfailing devotion, bravery and intelligence shown by so many animals – in this case 'animals' includes birds also. As more people keep dogs than any other pet, it is not surprising there should be so many instances where dogs have proved that they really are 'man's best friend'. However, cats, pigeons, horses, rats, monkeys, pigs and even an elephant have also been acclaimed as heroes.

I enjoyed writing this book and it has only served to reinforce my respect for the animals which share our world. I am also delighted that part of the royalties will go to the People's Dispensary for Sick Animals – especially as so many of the animals mentioned, were awarded the PDSA's Dickin Medal.

Chapter One

A Helping Paw

REMARKABLE STORIES concerning animals have been told throughout the ages. From elephants to pigeons, dogs to chimpanzees, cats to pigs – their courage, compassion and intelligence have left many people filled with admiration. These heroes, besides helping other animals, are also quick to 'lend a helping paw' to their human friends. For many people a particular pet holds a treasured place in their hearts, but in Ray Wakelin's case his two dogs must be equally special to him. When he decided to take these German Shepherds, Rommel and Zeus, for a walk one cold January night, he little realized that they were about to save his life. Fortuitously, he had also offered to exercise a friend's dog called Zak.

In the sub zero temperatures Ray suddenly slipped and knocked himself unconscious. As he lay on the freezing ground, Rommel and Zeus snuggled up either side of him, preventing his body temperature from dropping to dangerously low levels. Zak, meanwhile, frantically licked Ray's face and after almost an hour succeeded in bringing him round.

Although he could not feel his arms or legs, Ray somehow managed to stagger to a telephone box where he alerted friends who came to pick him and the dogs up. Ray was eventually revived with hot drinks and later received hospital treatment for blurred vision suffered as a result of his ordeal. When the Royal Society for the Prevention of Cruelty to Animals heard about the incident they decided to present the dogs with awards, in recognition of their 'intelligence and courage'. It was said that if the dogs had not acted as they did, Ray could have died.

This is just one of the many examples of how animals can literally save lives. On another occasion, a standard poodle suffered six nearly fatal bites from a rattlesnake in order to protect his young owner. And there was the Burmese cat whose actions saved forty-four people in an apartment fire.

In man's ancient legends animals too have earned their place. The village of Beddgelert (Grave of Gelert) in Wales reputedly owes its name to a wolfhound belonging to Prince Llewelyn. The story dates back to the 13th century. Legend has it that one day, on his return from a hunting expedition, the prince found Gelert covered in blood. Alarmed at this sight, the prince rushed to check on his infant son in a nearby chamber and discovered blood-stained sheets amidst a scene of chaos. There appeared to be no sign of the child, and believing Gelert had killed his son, the prince drew his sword and immediately destroyed the dog. But the wolfhound's dying cry woke the child who was in fact hidden, unharmed, beneath blankets, and close by Prince Llewelyn found, to his horror, the body of a large wolf. Realizing that Gelert had actually defended the child by killing the wolf, the prince was full of remorse.

In the 19th century the story was retold in verses by William Spencer and today people visit Gelert's reputed grave, marked with a stone, in a meadow near Snowdon in North Wales.

Some people might not think of a pig as a particularly heroic animal, yet Priscilla would certainly prove them wrong. She won the American Humane Association's Stillman Award in 1984 for saving a boy from drowning.

Priscilla's owners and their friends had taken the three-month-old pet pig to a lake in Texas, where she ventured into the water wearing her purple harness and leash. A young retarded boy, also in the water, got into difficulties and started to panic, but his mother reacted quickly and shouted at him to grab the pig's leash. In the drama both the boy and Priscilla disappeared under the water, but the plucky pig soon struck out for the shore, towing the youngster behind her.

After the event Priscilla was declared a local heroine in Houston and later she even went on television, complete with eyeshadow. As a celebrity, she was driven by car to the University of Illinois to open the International Belly Flop Contest and received the honour of being elected the first member of the Texas Pet Hall of Fame.

The Stillman Award, which Priscilla received, is named after

Dr William O. Stillman, a past president of the American Humane Association. Everyone who knew him called him a true humanitarian and he spent a great deal of his life protecting animals from cruelty. In 1928 funds were left to the Association by Mrs Morris H. Vandergrift of Philadelphia. The income was to be used to purchase medals, which were then awarded not only to animals whose actions saved human lives but to people who put themselves at great risk in order to save animals.

The Association itself was founded in 1877 and is dedicated to the prevention of cruelty and exploitation of children and animals. In its formative years, besides helping children, the Association pressed for laws to protect animals in transportation and also to help them during natural disasters. It continues to be a voice for those unable to speak for themselves and provides educational material for students and teachers.

The Ken-L Ration award programme has been honouring acts of canine bravery in America for thirty-four years. The Quaker Oats Company, makers of Ken-L Ration pet food, collects nominations from the media, government officials and members of the public. The list of candidates is narrowed down and dog lovers all over the nation are then asked to vote for the 'Dog Hero'. The winner receives a medal complete with red, white and blue ribbon and a year's supply of dog food. Ken-L Ration also sponsor a 'Dog Hero Week' in America which takes place the first week in March every year. This time is set aside especially to encourage dog owners to recognize everyday acts of canine heroism and people do various things to celebrate: they can take their town dogs to the country for a day or extend their dog's daily walk by fifteen minutes, for example.

The first co-winners of the prestigious Ken-L award were Champ and Buddy, who drew attention to the plight of a man in an isolated warehouse who was pinned under a scraper tyre that weighed more than a ton. In 1988 the award went to a six-year-old Doberman pinscher called Jet from Sepulveda, California. She saved the life of her owner, Candy Sangster, who had slipped into a diabetic coma. Instead of staying by her owner's side, Jet seemed to understand that Candy needed help, so she left the Sangster's home and found her way into a neighbour's yard. There she drew attention to herself by barking and, because of her agitation, the neighbour realized that something was wrong and called for assistance.

Having an animal as a friend brings hours of happiness, as countless pet owners can testify, but one young girl had a special reason to value her playmate's friendship – the animal became her lifesaver.

Dick and Lynda Veit had a Newfoundland dog called Villa who became close friends with Andrea Andersen, the girl who lived next door. One day, in February 1983, a blizzard allowed Andrea and her sisters to miss school. After much persuasion, their mother agreed that they could go and play in the snow near the house, but after a while only Andrea remained outside. Suddenly, a powerful gust of wind blew the small girl into a deep snowdrift only yards from the sea. She struggled in vain to get back to the house, but her efforts and cries for help went unheard. Only Villa picked up the familiar voice amidst the howling gale and jumping a five-foot fence, rushed to the rescue.

At first Villa circled Andrea, trampling down the snow with her large paws, then she lowered her head so that Andrea could reach round her neck. Villa dragged Andrea from the drift until she could stand up and then led her back to safety. When the Veits heard how Villa had saved Andrea they realized just what a heroine she was and rewarded her with a juicy steak for supper. Later, Villa received another reward – a Ken-L Ration medal for 'outstanding loyalty and intelligence' at a ceremony in Washington.

Another hero, who saved his owner's life, was accidentally left behind in the mountains as rescuers took his master to safety.

In 1975 Mark Cooper set off from his home in California on a trip to Sierra Nevada taking his faithful dog, a German Shepherd called Zorro, with him. Whilst walking in the mountains Mark lost his balance and toppled into a ravine. He fell approximately 85 feet, was knocked out in the process and landed in a stream below. As he slowly regained consciousness, he became aware of Zorro pulling him out of the water and up the steep, rocky slope.

Fortunately, some friends found Mark and went to get help whilst Zorro lay on top of his master, keeping him warm. The next day a helicopter was brought in and Mark was flown to safety, but unfortunately during the turmoil Zorro was forgotten. Messages were broadcast and subsequently volunteers set out to search for the dog. Eventually to everyone's relief, he was spotted guarding Mark's backpack. He was joyously reunited with his owner. In 1976 Zorro was honoured as Ken-L Ration's 'Dog Hero Of The Year' and proudly received his medal for intelligence and devotion.

Another canine hero honoured at a ceremony in London was Toby, a seven-year-old Dachshund/Jack Russell cross who saved ten people in flats threatened by a gas leak. Toby drew attention to the leak by persistent barking which made his owner follow him. He led her to the flats in Basingstoke and she then alerted the Gas Board who evacuated the area. PRO-Dogs decided to honour Toby's actions by presenting him with a medal, but Toby proved to be a reluctant hero and had to be dragged on stage to receive his award.

Rusty, a cross-bred Collie bitch, saved toddler Philip Stevens from some four-legged threats – a stampeding herd of cows. Rusty's owner, James Craig, aged twelve, from St. Austell in Cornwall, was playing with his friend and Philip in some fields. Philip's mother was nearby, but after a while she and the two older boys moved further away, leaving Philip playing happily near a gap in the hedge between fields where some cows were grazing. Suddenly something seemed to frighten the cows, who stampeded and to everyone's horror appeared to be heading straight for the gap where Philip was. They knew they could not reach the toddler in time, but Rusty was already racing down the field, barking furiously. She just made it and, rushing at the cows, managed to divert them although she received a painful kick on the shoulder. For her bravery and resourcefulness Rusty was given a medal and certificate from the PDSA at a special function organized in her honour.

Another dog also proved he could quickly sum up a situation and save his owner's life. One day James Rigg decided to take his black and white Border Collie, Tripper, out for a walk along a secluded beach at Pobbles Bay. Whilst walking, James suffered an epileptic fit and collapsed, face down, in the sand. Tripper immediately sensed the emergency and realizing his owner needed help, raced half a mile along the beach until he found a party of holiday-makers.

Tripper did everything he could to make the people follow

him and, guessing something was wrong by his agitated behaviour, they decided to go along with him. The holiday-makers found the dog's owner unconscious, hastily contacted the coastguards and later a rescue helicopter from the RAF flew James to hospital where he made a full recovery. It was said that if Tripper had not acted as promptly or as thoughtfully as he did, James could have died. The family made a great fuss of their 'hero' who happily posed for photographers after the event and was subsequently awarded an RSPCA Plaque for intelligence and courage, inscribed with his name.

Sheena, the German Shepherd pet of the Humphrey family living in Bolton, is a 'ladies dog', according to Mrs Margaret Humphrey: when her six foot two inch husband took the dog to training classes, Sheena dragged him straight out again in an effort to be reunited with Mrs Humphrey. So Margaret Humphrey took over Sheena's training, and later she was very glad she had done so, for on one occasion it was not a toy Sheena was retrieving – it was her son!

Margaret's children, Susan, Sarah and four-year-old Brian Humphrey were playing with the dog near a river bank when Brian lost his balance and fell into the water. He was quickly swept away by the fast flowing current and as neither of his sisters could swim, they were utterly helpless. Suddenly Sarah had an idea and kneeling down to Sheena, pointed to her brother in the water and gave the command 'Fetch!'.

The German Shepherd plunged into the water and swam strongly towards Brian, reaching him less than thirty yards from a weir and waterfall. She grabbed his sweater and struck out for the bank, finally being hauled out by a security guard from a local factory who had spotted the drama. In this instance, the family had very good reason to thank Sheena for paying attention during her visits to obedience classes; for what is usually a game, turned out to be a matter of life or death.

Hachiko, an Akita dog, was famous throughout Japan when his story became known. Every day Hachiko accompanied his master Dr Eisaburo Ueno to the Shibuya railway station in Tokyo and was there every night to greet him on his return. One day, in 1925, Dr Ueno tragically died whilst at work at Tokyo University. That night Hachiko was at the station as usual and waited until midnight in vain for his master to return. Day after day for the following ten years Hachiko went to the station at the usual time to wait hopefully for his master. When the dog died in 1935, a small bronze statue was erected at the Shibuya station, and this rapidly became a popular meeting place for couples. Subsequently, every year on 8 April, a special ceremony takes place in honour of his memory and during centenary celebrations there even appeared a look-alike dog who was made stationmaster for a day.

Man has long described the dog as his faithful friend and none could be more so than the small terrier called Bobby who lived in Scotland. Greyfriars Bobby had his story made into a film by Walt Disney and his statue became a well-known landmark.

John Gray, known as 'Auld Jock', was a shepherd whose flock roamed the Pentland Hills just south of Edinburgh. Jock and his dog Bobby were often seen in the Greyfriars Dining Rooms in Candlemaker Row, where they would be welcomed by the owner John Traill and given a tasty meal.

In 1858 the old shepherd died and was buried at Greyfriars Kirkyard. Bobby refused to leave the grave and even when evicted from the churchyard, the dog somehow contrived to find a way back in. In bad weather Bobby sheltered under a broken tombstone near his master's grave and at one o'clock each day he trotted over to the Greyfriars Dining Rooms where he received a meal from his friend. The Traill family tried to take him home on numerous occasions but each time Bobby returned promptly to his master's grave where he stayed day and night.

Nine years after Bobby had started his vigil, he was arrested by the police as an 'unlicensed vagrant' and was in danger of being sentenced to death. His friend Mr Traill appeared in court with him accused of 'harbouring' the dog, but when the Lord Provost Sir William Chambers heard the story he immediately undertook to pay for a licence for Bobby every year for the rest of the dog's life. He also had a collar made with the inscription: 'Greyfriars Bobby, from the Lord Provost 1867. Licensed.' which can be seen today in Edinburgh's City Museum at Huntly House.

Bobby died in 1872 after spending fourteen years at his master's graveside, and was buried near Greyfriars Church. The faithful dog's resting place is now a flower bed near the main entrance to the church, and American admirers of Bobby paid for a headstone to be placed over Auld Jock's grave. Nearby in Candlemaker Row a drinking fountain and bronze statue in Bobby's memory was erected by a leading figure in Victorian society, Baroness Burdett-Coutts, and quickly became one of Edinburgh's landmarks.

The phrase 'one man and his dog' could have been coined especially for a Czech man and his dog Antis, for the two were devoted to each other. When Jan Bozdech rescued the homeless, starving German Shepherd puppy little did he know that the dog would later save his life on two occasions, and become the first foreign dog to win the Dickin Medal.

Jan joined the French Air Force during the Second World War and after numerous escapades during which he and Antis were shot down and then rescued, the pair arrived safely in England where Jan was accepted for training by the RAF. After the war Jan and Antis returned to Czechoslovakia but eventually, to escape the communist authorities and leaving his family behind, Jan made an attempt to cross the Iron Curtain through to the West. Jan travelled with two other men, who at first were not keen to have a dog along, but when Antis proved how valuable he was at detecting enemy patrols, they relented. At one point, the men had to cross a river under cover of darkness and in the strong current Jan lost his footing and hit his head on a boulder. Antis grabbed hold of his jacket and the two managed to reach the bank. However, Jan's other colleagues needed to be found, as all had been separated whilst crossing the river and Jan knew that without his friends to help and guide him he was lost, so he sent Antis to 'seek'. The dog returned after successfully locating both men, and all three were able to continue their journey.

Their troubles, however, were still not over and once again Antis proved himself to be a life-saver. As the mist descended, the dog was placed on guard on a rock overlooking the path and although Jan and his friends heard nothing, Antis pounced on a border guard who was in danger of discovering the men. Eventually Jan and Antis were able to complete their journey safely across the border and once again found themselves in England.

Antis was quarantined for six months where he pined for Jan and became seriously ill. Jan had been unable to visit due to a slipped cartilage but when he heard news of his dog's unhappiness he arranged to be transferred by the medical authorities to be near the kennels, so that he could see Antis. As soon as the dog heard Jan say the familiar words 'Looking for someone?' Antis' spirits rose and he started to improve.

Under the conditions of re-enlistment Jan had to accept a lower rank and subsequent loss of pay, and found himself unable to meet the twenty-five shillings per week fees for quarantine. Fortunately, the PDSA came to the rescue on learning of the dog's history, and paid the fees. In January 1949 Antis and Jan were reunited and in March of that year the dog received the Dickin Medal from Lord Wavell, who congratulated Antis personally.

When Antis was thirteen years old he became ill and although treatment from the vet seemed to improve matters temporarily, it appeared he would never fully recover. Jan wrote to the PDSA who advised him that the kindest thing would be to put Antis out of his misery, so on 11 August 1953 Jan carried his dog to the operating table at the sanatorium at Ilford. Jan stayed with Antis and stroked his head as the dog was painlessly injected. Antis was later buried at the Animal Cemetery at Ilford and the words on his grave are as follows:–

> There is an old belief
> That on some solemn shore
> Beyond the sphere of grief
> Dear friends shall meet once more.

Jan has never owned another dog.

Chapter Two

Above and Beyond the Call of Duty

WHEN GUIDE DOGS for the blind were first introduced the public reacted against the idea of animals 'working'. However, over the years attitudes began to change and now we also have organizations such as Hearing Dogs for the Deaf, Dogs for the Disabled and Helping Hands – using capuchin monkeys – besides the P.A.T. (PRO-Dogs Active Therapy) dogs who bring so much pleasure to those normally deprived of animal companionship.

The P.A.T. scheme was launched in 1983 by the PRO-Dogs charity – an organization aimed at promoting a positive attitude towards our canine friends. PRO-Dogs was founded in 1976 by Lesley Scott Ordish and the charity endeavours to counteract anti-dog campaigns and supplies well-researched details about the advantages of having dogs in society.

Under the P.A.T. scheme, volunteers belonging to PRO-Dogs and covered by the appropriate insurance, offer to take their dogs to visit people who would otherwise be deprived of animal contact, for example those in nursing homes, hospices and other institutions. To be registered under the P.A.T. scheme a dog must pass a temperament test and then he is allowed to wear a special disc on his collar. The happiness that these animals bring is clearly seen on the faces of many elderly, mentally disturbed, disabled and infirm people.

It was during a training exercise that one P.A.T. dog called Jacob came to the rescue when his owner was attacked. Jacob was practising an 'out-of-sight stay' when his owner Mrs Betty Harris was punched in the back and thrown to the ground. Her attacker, thinking she was alone, tried to snatch her handbag, but Betty's cries of 'Jacob come!' brought her German

Shepherd bounding up. The man tried to escape with the bag but the dog gave chase.

Betty rushed home and told her husband what had happened. He was just about to go looking for Jacob, when to their relief the dog came trotting through the door. Although cut on the mouth, he had managed to retrieve his owner's handbag, and Mrs Harris later said that if Jacob had not come to the rescue, she dreaded to think what might have happened.

Jacob's obedience has won him numerous rosettes at competitions and on one occasion he even remained sitting in the rain outside a shop when his owner dashed past him and raced home, completely forgetting she had left him there! At their annual award dinner, PRO-Dogs presented Jacob with a medal as 'Pet of the Year' and his charming personality and co-operative nature made him a special hit with photographers.

When looking for instances of dogs helping their owners, the working guide dogs for the blind provide many excellent examples. Modern guide dog training started in Germany after the First World War. Mrs Dorothy Eustis, an American German Shepherd dog breeder living in Switzerland, trained a German Shepherd bitch called Kiss (later named Buddy) to be the first American guide dog for a man named Morris Frank. Mrs Eustis eventually returned to the United States and in 1929 she and Morris founded a guide dog school called 'The Seeing Eye' in order to train more dogs and people.

Meanwhile, Morris Frank and Buddy toured the country, fund-raising and giving talks. As Buddy proved herself time and again, so Morris Frank's confidence grew. On one occasion Buddy dragged her master up an embankment to escape a pair of runaway horses, and in another instance she threw her weight in front of him to stop him falling down an open lift-shaft – after he had ignored her warning signals! Even during play, Buddy was always aware of possible dangers and once, when Morris grew tired whilst swimming in a lake and started to lose his bearings, Buddy came to the rescue and pulled him to shore. The dog even saved the day when an intruder tried to break into the Frank home. Buddy crouched beside the window as it was being forced open, but instead of barking to warn the burglar off, the dog employed a more effective and unique deterrent, causing the intruder to beat a somewhat hasty and painful retreat.

After years of dedicated service the faithful dog died, but the name 'Buddy' was reserved and could only be used for Morris's guide dogs.

In 1930 Miss Muriel Crooke and Mrs Rosamund Bond asked Dorothy Eustis to help them set up a guide dogs training scheme in Britain. Mrs Eustis agreed and sent one of her trainers to England, where work began, using a rented piece of land and a garage in Wallasey, Cheshire. At first many people objected to the idea of a dog working (there were no dogs helping the police, army or RAF at that time) and trainers were often abused or stopped in the street by angry members of the public. Some people said that the work was cruel and useless, but when they saw the difference that having a guide dog made to a blind person and they saw that the dogs were happy in their work, opinions began to change.

In 1941 a large house and grounds at Leamington Spa, Warwickshire, was bought and later a proper breeding and 'puppy-walking' centre was established. This came about because one man, Mr John Gray, was so impressed by a particular guide dog he saw negotiating busy morning traffic and trains in St. Albans.

Sweep was discovered by Mr Derek Freeman, manager at the Association, on a deserted farm near Leamington Spa. Before the breeding programme was established, guide dogs often came from unlikely sources. It was thought that the dog was a cross between a German Shepherd and a black and white Border Collie; he had no owner, no home, no pedigree and no name. Despite his dubious start, Sweep proved to be a first-class guide dog. Although he had never been off the farm before (according to a neighbour), he took traffic, crowds, shops and new commands all in his stride. Eventually he qualified and was placed with Mike Tetley – becoming Mike's first guide dog.

Whilst working, Sweep devised his own way of clearing a path through a crowd of talking, dawdling women. He would come up behind them, put his nose between their legs, lift their skirts and blow. If that failed, he would put his shoulder against their knees and push them gently out of the way. Mike taught his dog various commands such as 'Find the Post Office' and 'Find Boots – the chemist'. However, when Mike moved from Luton to St. Albans he had difficulty teaching

Sweep to 'Find Boots'. As far as Sweep was concerned, 'Boots' was in Luton and you could not have 'Boots' in St. Albans too. A guide dog's training incorporates the word 'Busy' to encourage the dog to relieve itself. On one occasion when Mike was in a public lavatory he realized that Sweep also needed to go and instructed him to 'Get Busy'. Sweep immediately stepped forward and cocked his leg in exactly the right place – to the absolute amazement of the attendant.

Off duty, Sweep enjoyed playing and was once found lying in bed with a hat and dress on – Mike's children had disguised him as the wolf from *Little Red Riding Hood*. He could also be quite an escapologist. He managed to clear an eight-and-a-half-foot fence with the help of a packing case which he found and pushed into position, about five feet from the obstacle. To make sure that the presence of the case was not a coincidence, Mike moved it away, but Sweep carefully replaced it and jumped the fence again.

It was Sweep's work that so impressed John Gray and prompted him to organize regular collections for the Guide Dogs For The Blind Association at his place of work, the Diamond Corporation in London. One day Mr Gray suggested to his directors that the company should match what the staff had collected. In fact the company went much further than that. In 1969 the Board of Directors agreed to give £35,000 for the purchase of Tollgate House in Leamington Spa. The guide dogs were considered a suitable charity to support because to sort diamonds the staff needed excellent eyesight, so they fully appreciated the value of sight.

Puppies bred by the Guide Dogs For The Blind Association spend their first year with 'puppy-walkers' – families who volunteer to look after them, introduce them to traffic, shops, buses, crowds and teach them the basic commands. The dogs are then returned to the Association for further months of intensive training before being matched with a blind person. During training they are taught how to be 'intelligently disobedient' – for example, disregarding a command to cross a road when a car is coming, and also to think of themselves as being about six feet tall and four feet wide, in order to negotiate obstacles like low branches and scaffolding for themselves and their owners.

To many, the fact that a dog can lead a blind person seems

incredible enough, but when that person is also deaf and mute a quite exceptional dog is called for. Such a dog was Nelson, a male Labrador.

Normally a blind person gives verbal commands to his dog but for Clark Stevens this was not possible. Nelson underwent training in the normal way except that vocal commands were omitted and special signals were used instead. Nelson rose to the challenge and soon Clark and his dog were going through their paces together. Everyone was delighted at how quickly Nelson adapted to non-vocal communication and responded well to hand signals, gestures and physical praise.

Clark, meanwhile, had to use a whistle to practise 'recall' signals, although he had no idea what a whistle sounded like. He also had to learn how to snap his fingers to make a loud noise – something most people would take for granted, but how do you tell if yours is a 'failed' snap when you cannot hear anything anyway? It was made clear to Clark and his wife Liz that if at any time during the training the safety aspect was in doubt, the project would be abandoned. However it soon became evident that Clark and Nelson had developed a special rapport and everyone was delighted at the excellent communication which developed between this remarkable pair.

People who are blind have certainly benefited from their faithful guide dogs and those who are deaf, and lucky enough to have a canine helper, are also realizing how invaluable an animal assistant can be.

The American Humane Association piloted the first Hearing Dog programme in 1976, with a centre being established a year later in San Francisco. The aim of the scheme was to train dogs to act as 'hearing ears' for deaf people by alerting them to everyday sounds, thereby offering them a greater degree of independence. As news of the work spread, a similar scheme was set up in Britain in 1982. All the dogs used are unwanted animals, usually chosen from rescue homes. Their sizes range from Chihuahua to Irish Wolfhound, although the majority are most likely to be cross-breeds of a small to medium height and between eight months to two years old.

The most important prerequisites for a Hearing Dog, are friendly disposition, intelligence and inquisitiveness. Once selected, the dog undergoes two weeks of further tests with a trainer to confirm suitability. Veterinary examinations are also necessary before the dog completes a four-month training course – kindness, patience and reward being the methods used to instruct the dogs. Towards the end of the course, verbal commands are replaced by hand signals in order to assist the deaf person who has trouble formulating speech.

Following training, the dog is taken to its new home by the placement counsellor, who then continues to visit for approximately seven to ten days to ensure that both dog and recipient are happy and working well together. A Hearing Dog is allocated a distinctive orange collar and lead and also benefits from free veterinary treatment, besides being allowed to travel free of charge on London Transport, the National Bus Company, British Rail and British Airways internal flights.

A Hearing Dog costs £2,500 to train. The dog is taught to respond to the sounds chosen by the new owner, such as an alarm clock, a whistling kettle, oven timer or a knock at the door. The dog can even be instructed to fetch a deaf mother when her baby cries.

The first British Hearing Dog was Favour – chosen when he was a one-year-old stray at the National Canine Defence League Kennels. In 1986 he was awarded the PRO-Dogs 'Devotion to Duty' gold medal for his help in demonstrating the pioneering Hearing Dogs scheme in Britain. Besides giving such valuable help, a Hearing Dog also offers companionship and a feeling of security to many people living alone. In some cases a Hearing Dog can even save a life.

In America, one Hearing Dog called Sheena threw herself between her owner and a speeding car. Her deaf owner, Hannah Merker, was day-dreaming and did not notice her dog's signals and, of course, could not hear the warning shouts of passers-by. After spending a week in a veterinary hospital, Sheena was re-united with the grateful Hannah. An additional irony was that the animal had been selected from a rescue home to become a Hearing Dog only the day before she was due to be put to sleep.

Another American lady called Elizabeth Smith has a tiny helper in the shape of a part Terrier, part Chihuahua cross, called Chico. What he lacks in size, Chico makes up for in enthusiasm – waking his owner up in the morning by leaping on her. On one ocasion, whilst travelling on a bus, Chico refused to settle and his behaviour eventually drew attention to the fact that the roof of the bus was on fire. The dog is so well trained in fact, that when a telephone on stage rang during a play he was attending with his owner, Chico tried to take his mistress to the phone. He was most indignant when she refused to follow him!

Robbie and Moley are two Hearing Dogs in Britain whose owners give talks on the benefits these animals bring. Moley accompanies her owner, Mrs Betty Roesler, wherever she goes, including church, and on one occasion at the Abbey on Iona in Scotland, Moley impressed everyone with her impeccable behaviour. When Betty stood up for the hymns, so did Moley!

Mrs Shirley Cooper's dog, Robbie, enjoys going to the talks that Shirley gives; especially at the end of the talk when the clapping starts. He knows that tea and cake usually follow and gives everyone his most appealing look. Although Robbie has never been called upon to literally save Shirley's life, as she says, '. . . Robbie saves my day, every day . . . I know that some people think that £2,500 is a lot to train a dog, but believe me, if you were deaf and had one of the dogs given to you, you would then know they are worth every penny.'

Another dog deserves to be mentioned for her efforts in helping the deaf. Josie, a black and white Border Collie, achieved fame when she appeared on the children's television programme *Blue Peter*, after raising £2,175.51 for their 'Lend An Ear Appeal'. Josie is typical of the many animals who regularly go on sponsored walks or aid their owners in some way to raise money for charities, playing their part to help others, both animal and human, who are less fortunate .

Dogs, of course, feature widely in helping mankind, but other animals can also play a vital role. In America, Dr Mary Joan Willard was curious to see whether a monkey could be taught to help a paralysed person. In 1979 the Paralyzed Veterans of America awarded Dr Willard her first major grant and the non-profit making organization Helping Hands: Simian Aides for the Disabled was established.

Dr Willard decided to use Cebus monkeys, commonly called capuchins (or organ grinder monkeys). These animals seemed ideal as they could live for about thirty years and would be about the right size; weighing around five pounds and standing less than two feet tall.

Helping Hands now aims to breed its own monkeys for the programme and from around eight weeks of age the animals are raised by foster families (who are not required to teach the monkey any tasks). Monkeys live with these caring families so that by the time they are about three years old, they are sociable and affectionate. The animals then undergo months of specialized training – based on the work of B. F. Skinner, an eminent psychologist – before being placed with a quadriplegic.

The monkeys are formidably bright and quickly learn to respond to spoken commands such as 'Fetch' or 'Change', as well as visual instructions from the laser-pointer. They can also use their intelligence to test their owners, as one lady found out.

Sue Strong's capuchin, Henrietta (Henri to her friends), occasionally dims the lights when Sue is reading, knowing that Sue will then have to ask her to turn them back up – and so give the monkey a reward for performing her task correctly. Another smart monkey discovered, during a training session, how to trip an electric eye with a piece of its bedding in order to receive repeated rewards.

When not helping Sue by performing various tasks, Henri's antics are a constant diversion: she tries to peer into neighbours' windows, draws on a pad or throws kisses at herself in the mirror. The monkeys enjoy outings just as much as their owners and Sue takes Henri to the park when the weather permits. Another treat for Henri is a car ride. Sue's helper drives, whilst Henri is allowed to hand the money to toll-booth attendants.

Capuchins have a tendency to be loving and very loyal to those they regard as members of their troupe, which includes their owners, family members and part-time helpers. They can also be fastidiously clean and one trainer reported that some of the monkeys did not even like eating bananas because it meant getting their hands dirty – the fruit had to be wrapped in napkins instead.

It has been suggested that money used to further the work of Helping Hands would be better spent developing robotics to aid the disabled. However, as one man pointedly remarked, 'Robots won't play', and although a monkey might not suit everyone, there is no doubt that they bring a new dimension into the lives of many disabled people. In fact, the requests for simian aides in America far outstrips the supply at the moment, and following the success of Helping Hands, similar programmes in Canada, Argentina and Israel are now underway.

In Britain, a charity called Dogs for the Disabled was set up in 1986 by Mrs Frances Hay. As with the Hearing Dogs for the Deaf, Mrs Hay has used unwanted animals which might otherwise have had to be destroyed. The idea for such a scheme came about when she realized just how much her dog Kim was helping in her day-to-day routine.

Some of the dogs trained by this charity are used to help people overcome specific disabilities, whilst other dogs with a particularly sensitive, affectionate nature serve as companions in residential homes or to people with limited ability. The moral support that a dog gives can work wonders; one disabled lady felt confident enough to go on holiday by herself for the first time in fourteen years, whilst another paralyzed woman lifted her arm for the first time in seven years in order to stroke her dog.

Poppy, a beautiful King Charles cross-breed, was the victim of a car accident before being nursed back to health by one of the charity's trainers. Once recovered, Poppy joined the scheme and recently appeared on television, demonstrating her various capabilities such as opening a door, turning on a light, retrieving the post and picking up a pen. Poppy's owner, Amanda, said in the interview that she certainly felt more secure having a dog at home – and Poppy endorsed their togetherness by stopping for a quick cuddle.

The animals are able to assist with many household tasks and one lady had every reason to thank her canine helper when she suffered a stroke at home. The dog opened the door and fetched the telephone, enabling her to summon assistance. Without the dog's help the woman could have died.

People travelling by train in South Africa in the 1880s were initially alarmed by the sight of one particular signalman called Jack. Their consternation probably arose because Jack was a baboon.

Mr James Edwin Wide had left England to settle in South Africa and was employed by the Cape Government Railways. Whilst working on the construction of the railway from Uitenhage to Graaff-Reinet, Mr Wide was involved in an accident that resulted in the loss of both legs. He was subsequently given the job of signalman at Uitenhage and decided to teach his pet baboon, Jack, various tasks of general assistance. Besides pumping water from a well and helping with occasional gardening jobs, Jack learnt to operate the train signals under Mr Wide's supervision. The baboon quickly learnt that one blast from a train's whistle meant pulling down a certain lever and he would look to his owner to confirm this action. Mr Wide would indicate that Jack was correct by raising a finger and pointing to the lever.

Jack soon became quite proficient at his duties and would pull the required lever and then rush to the window to make sure that the signal arm had functioned and to watch the train go past. As news of this unusual signalman spread, trains slowed down at the signal box to enable passengers to see the baboon in action, and one day the supervisor of the Uitenhage railway section came to investigate.

He was so impressed with Jack's efficiency that Mr Wide was officially informed that his pet had been made assistant signalman and placed on the railway's payroll. From then on, Jack received wages of 9d. a day plus half a bottle of beer on Saturdays and continued to do his job, without a single accident, until he died in 1890.

Chapter Three

Wartime Heroics

DURING THE First World War an estimated eight million horses lost their lives and in the Second World War countless mules worked tirelessly alongside the Chindits in the jungles of South East Asia. In the two World Wars many soldiers' lives were saved by the courageous efforts of the mine detecting dogs but perhaps more unusual are those whose lives have been saved by feathered heroes, like pigeons. Whether it is right or wrong to use animals to help us in wartime will probably continue to be a subject for debate. However, the fact remains that many animals were 'enlisted' to help their country and it is ironic that some dogs which were once unwanted pets in rescue homes, should then be called upon to face the perils of war – many of them saving human lives.

In 1916 a War Dog School was set up at Shoeburyness and many recruits came from the Battersea Dogs' Home. Numerous animals were used as messengers – because of their speed and ability to negotiate difficult terrain. In this area alone, the lives of many military runners were saved. The Airedale breed proved very popular in this type of work, as the dogs were found to be highly trainable, with the added advantages of strength and stamina. One Airedale called Jack became a hero of the Great War when he saved a whole British battalion by carrying a crucial message back to base.

In the Second World War, British dogs were employed to carry ammunition, seek out enemy positions and guard vital suppplies, amongst other numerous tasks. Again, many of the animals who risked their lives came from the Battersea Dogs' Home. This now famous rescue centre was originally founded in 1860 in Holloway by Mrs Mary Tealby. Queen Victoria took a keen interest in the work being done there to help the plight of stray dogs and in 1862 Charles Dickens wrote an article about the home. As the kennels grew, so did complaints from the neighbours about the noise, and after some ten years the dogs' home moved to Battersea Fields – a place notorious for prizefights and duels.

Nowadays the animals reside in heated kennels waiting hopefully, but sometimes in vain, for a new owner from amongst the 100,000 people who visit the home annually. Over a hundred years ago one kennel was named after a particular benefactress and this practice still continues today – the plaque erected bearing the donor's or his favourite pet's name.

Two dogs won Dickin Medals for doing something many people would think twice about – parachute jumping. Brian, a cross-bred German Shepherd was serving with the 13th battalion of the Airborne Regiment and was awarded his medal after making the necessary number of jumps to qualify as a paratrooper.

Rob, a black and white Welsh Cattle Collie with a black patch over one eye, served with the SAS in North Africa and Italy. He seemed to relish jumping and would leap out of the plane without a moment's hesitation, landing with a perfect parachute roll. He quickly became known by the men as 'paradog' and made over twenty parachute landings, lying perfectly still until his handler caught up with him and removed the harness. The men's work was highly dangerous but Rob always kept close guard, warning them of any imminent risk. Rob received his award from Viscount De L'Isle and Dudley before returning to his farm home after the war. There, he immediately settled back into the routine of helping with the hens and acting as nursemaid to his owner's young son. However, rounding up the cows now became a problem for Rob, as rather than following the cattle to keep them together, the dog insisted on trying to lead them from the front! Rob's owners decided to give their hero an honourable retirement and the dog spent the rest of his days peacefully as a household pet.

Dickin Medals, like the ones presented to Brian and Rob, were given by the People's Dispensary for Sick Animals to mark outstanding achievements and exceptional bravery during the war. The award, which quickly became known as the animals' V.C., bears the words: 'For gallantry we also serve', and the ribbons are brown, green and blue, symbolizing animal heroics on land, sea and air.

The bronze medal was named after Mrs Maria Dickin CBE, the founder of the PDSA, who opened the first dispensary in 1917 in spite of great difficulties. The PDSA aims to provide free veterinary care for any sick or injured animal whose owner cannot afford private fees and the Dispensary is now the largest veterinary practice in Britain.

Patrol dogs were regularly used in the war to lead small groups of soldiers across dangerous territory and then give silent warnings as to the direction of the enemy. A cross-bred Collie called Bob, who won the Dickin Medal, was on such a patrol when he suddenly froze. The men waited, heard nothing and after a few minutes wanted to press on. The dog, however, adamantly refused to move, and seconds later the enemy came into view only 200 yards ahead. Bob's actions certainly saved his party, the enemy being much nearer than the men realized, and they were able to successfully relay important information to their command.

Animal war heroes were to be found world-wide and it seems the Russian Air Force was no exception. Squadron Leader Nefedov used to take his dog Dootik with him on missions. On one occasion his plane was shot down by German fighters, resulting in all the crew being badly wounded. Their only hope of rescue seemed to be the dog and so a message was tied to his collar and Dootik, after much encouragement, set off on the difficult journey through enemy patrols. The desperate crew were overjoyed and relieved when at last they spotted the returning Dootik, proudly leading a rescue party.

During the war, police dogs played an important role in protecting ammunition dumps and aerodromes. One outstanding RAF police dog was Storm, a pure white German Shepherd, born in 1944. Storm was an 'instructor dog', as experience had shown that dogs under training learnt more effectively from others showing them what to do. Storm's excellence also made him ideal for the starring role in an RAF training film. The dog, like many other canines, was not without his own idiosyncrasies and he enjoyed nothing more than eating tarred gravel, despite constant dosing with emetics. He also had a mischievous streak in him and would sometimes use his 110-pound weight to pull his unsuspecting handler right off his feet.

Prince, also a German Shepherd, was a good all-rounder; able to pick out natives at a distance of approximately 200 yards and always obeying commands with a keen spirit. He was credited with eighteen arrests and frequently tackled thieves carrying weapons – sometimes there were as many as fourteen people – displaying unswerving courage and devotion.

Three Boxer dogs, Simmi, Ran and Rina, also deserve a mention for the dedicated way in which they carried out their duties. Simmi worked in Palestine during the Second World War. His work consisted mainly of night patrols in the Middle East and he had a total of eighty-six arrests to his credit. Simmi was trained to bring a man down and hold him until an arrest could be made, and on one occasion the man in question, a violent thief, headed towards a moving train. Simmi gave chase, pulling the man from the train, and succeeded in detaining him until help arrived.

Ran and Rina also regularly tackled thieves in the course of their duties. Rina tracked some natives for about two miles into the desert and although close to exhaustion, she managed to capture one man and hold him until her handler appeared. Ran came to the aid of his handler when he was knocked down by thieves. The five natives, all armed, had broken into an ammunition dump. As Ran's handler blew his whistle for assistance the thieves struck him, but Ran successfully held them off until help arrived and then managed to capture one of the thieves himself.

Mine detection was just another way in which dogs gave their assistance during the war. It was discovered that the dogs could detect mines made out of wood, glass, metal or plastic and so their help proved invaluable on numerous occasions. The dogs selected for this type of work obviously needed to be extremely intelligent and the following example proves the point.

During a training session, seventy-five mines were planted in a field and the dogs found them all except one. On later inspection however, it was revealed that the mine was very small and by mistake the explosive had been omitted. As the dogs were trained to find only those mines which would explode, they all passed with flying colours – demonstrating that there was no error on *their* part!

The Russians also used mine dogs and one animal called Zhucha, a mongrel, was considered so important that he used to travel by plane with his handler. Incredibly, he once detected a total of 2,000 mines in eighteen days.

The Council of the RSPCA awarded the most distinguished mine dogs with special collars inscribed with the words 'For Valour'. Some notable dogs were Texas, a yellow Labrador, who worked under continual gun fire on the Rhine crossing, and Bruce, a black Labrador, considered one of the most reliable animals in mine detection. Bruce once worked for three hours under very difficult conditions, checking an approach to the Reichswald forest and was also responsible for clearing a section of railway line, enabling important supplies to get through. There was also a Dalmation called Scamp who, whilst working under extremely hazardous conditions in a confined space, managed to find twenty-six mines and was officially praised for his outstanding devotion to duty.

A dog who won the Dickin Medal for his services, as well as an RSPCA award, was the mine dog Ricky. Ricky, alias Rex, was purchased by his owner Mrs Litchfield of Kent for 7s. 6d. when he was four months old. In 1944 the Welsh sheepdog met his handler, Maurice Yelding, at the Dog Training School and later Ricky was sent to Holland to help clear the verges on canal banks. At one point, a mine blew up only three feet away from him, wounding Ricky in the head. However, the brave dog did not panic, which could have endangered the rest of the party. Instead, he remained calm and kept on working successfully, finding several more mines. After the war, when Ricky was due to be released from duty, the military authorities offered his owner a high fee to keep Ricky in the service, but the offer was refused. The dog returned home and in May 1947 was awarded the Dickin Medal for his dedication and courage.

In the First World War the Canine Defence League launched an appeal for funds to help families of men serving in the Army, Navy and Air Force, to feed and license their pets. The public responded through their own pets, such as 'Brownie and Jock' who gave £1.2s.6d., and 'Glen – a happy civilian dog' who willingly donated 5s. This meant that soldiers' families could look forward to regular supplies of food for their animals

1. Champ and Buddy with Harvey and Anneliese Schmidt (see page 3). [*Ken-L Ration Dog Hero of the Year Awards. Quaker Oats*]

2. Villa with Andrea Anderson (see page 4). [*Ken-L Ration*]

3. Sheena with Brian Humphrey (see page 6). [*Sunday Express*]
4. Greyfriars Bobby (see page 7). [*The British Tourist Authority/ETB*]
5. Hachiko (see page 6). [*Chuken Hachiko dozo ijikai namiki sadahito jimusho*]

6. Jacob with Mrs Betty Harris (see page 10). [*Times Newspapers Ltd.*]
7. Buddy guiding Morris Frank (see page 11). [*The Seeing Eye*]
8. Sweep guiding Mike Tetley (see page 12). [*St. Dunstan's*]

9. Nelson with Clark Stevens and trainer (see page 14). [*The Guide Dogs for the Blind Association*]
10. Robbie, another Hearing Dog (see page 16). [*Mrs Shirley Cooper*]
11. Sheena, a Hearing Dog, with Hannah Merker (see page 15). [*Hannah Merker*]

12. Henri, a Helping Hands monkey, prepares a drink for Sue Strong (see page 17). [*Rita Nanni–Helping Hands*]

13. Jack the baboon, signalman, with James Edwin Wide (see page 18). [*South African Transport Services Museum*]

14. PDSA's Dickin Medal (see page 21). [*PDSA*]

15. Comanche at Fort Riley, Kansas (see page 25). [*The Kansas State Historical Society*]

16. GI Joe wearing his Dickin Medal (see page 27). [*PDSA*]
17. White Vision (see page 28). [*PDSA*]

18. Rats (see page 36). [*Mail Newspapers plc*]
19. Judy (see page 35). [*PDSA*]
20. Our Dumb Friends' League cats' and dogs' ambulance (see page 41). [*The Blue Cross Animal Welfare Society*]

and the League managed to pay for over 11,000 dog licences.

Today the National Canine Defence League maintains rescue centres throughout the country where they care for unwanted, lost or abandoned dogs. Where possible, caring homes are found for the animals, but as no healthy dog is ever destroyed, a certain number seem destined to remain at the kennels. The League now operates a Sponsored Dog scheme which enables those who would like a dog of their own, but are unable to have one for any reason, to visit regularly their chosen animal. In many cases it is also possible to groom and exercise your 'own' dog.

During the First World War, one dog's efforts played a vital part in the defence of the Allies' position at Verdun. Cross-bred Greyhound Satan was sent on an important mission which involved the evasion of gunfire as he made his way across no-man's-land to his handler's camp. Although the dog seemed, to those watching, to fly across the ground, he was nevertheless hit by a bullet. Satan collapsed, his back leg shattered, but on hearing his handler's voice encouraging him, he struggled on until he finally reached safety. The message he bore stated that help was on its way, and strapped to the dog's back were baskets containing two pigeons which enabled the men to pass back important information, thus saving Verdun.

German Shepherd dog Khan, later known as Rifleman Khan, won the Dickin Medal for saving his handler, Corporal J. Muldoon, from drowning.

Khan originally belonged to a Surrey family who offered his services during the war. The handsome dog was accepted by the Forces and sent for training before being placed with a battalion of the 6th Cameronians serving overseas. At one point Khan and Corporal Muldoon were crossing the sea to Walcheren when their boat capsized due to heavy shell-fire. The dog set off calmly to swim to shore but on reaching land, Khan could not find his handler. Muldoon could not swim and through the general noise and commotion, Khan heard the man's cries for help. Disregarding falling shells and the danger to his own life, Khan leapt back into the water and swam to Muldoon whom he then towed to the shore.

Whilst dogs featured widely in courageous war exploits, horses too, played their part, and Comanche's claim to fame must surely be unique – this horse survived the Battle of the

Little Bighorn. Comanche was one of the wild mustangs captured in about 1868 by the wild horse hunters and sold to the US army for 90 dollars. He and a number of other horses were taken to Fort Leavenworth, Kansas, before moving to the 7th Cavalry's encampment near Ellis, where Comanche soon became the favourite mount of Captain Myles Keogh. The 15-hands bay horse, with a small white star on his forehead, reputedly got his name from a soldier who said that the animal yelled like a Comanche on one occasion when an arrow pierced his right hind-quarter.

The horse was about fourteen years old when the Battle of the Little Bighorn took place on 25 June 1876. Some authorities believe that there were as many as 12,000 Indians, including 2,000 warriors in the area and every man in five companies of the 7th Cavalry was killed. After the fight, some horses were taken away by the Indians, but Comanche was so seriously injured (one bullet had passed straight through his neck) that he was left on the battlefield, where he was discovered still alive two days later. The horse was taken to Fort Lincoln, where he was too weak to walk, but following almost a year of careful attention and nursing, Comanche recovered.

Once he was fit, the horse was allowed the freedom of the post and used to wander over the parade grounds of Lincoln, without so much as a reprimand from a commanding officer. Some men later recounted how Comanche would stand outside the doors of the officers' quarters waiting for sugar lumps and often turned up at the canteen in the hope of receiving a bucket of beer. Also on several occasions, when the bugles called for squadron formation, the horse would trot to his old place in his master's troop.

On 10 April 1878 special orders were given, stating that Comanche should never be ridden again under any circumstances and that he was not to do work of any kind. Instead, the horse was paraded at ceremonies and each 25 June, an official regimental day of mourning, Comanche led Keogh's old troop, draped in black and with the stirrups reversed.

In 1888 the 7th Cavalry moved to Fort Riley and, after spending his remaining years peacefully, Comanche died in November 1891 aged about twenty-nine years. His body was preserved and now stands in a special glass case at the University of Kansas.

The Duke of Wellington's horse was another famous mount. Copenhagen's memory lives on at Stratfield Saye, where the present Duke still has mementos of the great horse. Copenhagen was not a large animal but he was the Duke of Wellington's favourite, and received his name because his mother was in Denmark when she was found to be in foal. He was a small, chestnut stallion, just over 15 hands high and although not very good at jumping, had tremendous endurance.

At the Battle of Waterloo against Napoleon, the Duke of Wellington rode Copenhagen from 6 a.m. until 11 p.m., making tours of inspection and galloping into the action. When the battle was over and the Duke had reached the inn at Waterloo, he at last dismounted. He went to pat Copenhagen but the horse lashed out, broke free and galloped off. However, the Duke had been very impressed by his mount and he declared that there may have been faster or better looking horses but as far as he was concerned, Copenhagen had no equal. The horse retired to Wellington's estate at Stratfield Saye where he was occasionally hunted by the Duke. When Copenhagen died in 1836, at the age of twenty-eight, he was buried with honours in the grounds of the house and a monument erected over his grave.

During the Second World War many different animals gave their services, including pigeons who played a most important role, carrying vital messages. Winged messengers were used as long ago as 650 BC by the Chinese, and in 1150 the Sultan of Baghdad filled capsules with notes of papyrus and strapped them to the birds' legs. Pigeons were also used to carry the news of Caesar's conquest and, later, Wellington's victory at Waterloo. Even today the Swiss Army Pigeon Corps employs some 30,000 birds for communication purposes in the event of a nuclear war. One of the most popular pigeons in the Second World War was GI Joe, who received the Dickin Medal and also visited the Tower of London.

GI Joe served with the US Forces in Italy. In October 1943 air support was requested by a British army division, to enable the strong German position at Colvi Vecchia to be broken. Allied pilots were preparing their planes for take off in order to bomb the town, when GI Joe arrived bearing his vital message. Apparently soldiers from the 169th Infantry Brigade had succeeded in capturing the village and, had the bombs been dropped as planned, a disaster would have occurrred. The pigeon had flown twenty miles from the British 10th Army HQ, in the same number of minutes. Had he arrived even five minutes later, it would have been impossible to stop the pilots taking off and at least a hundred allied soldiers would have been bombed by their own planes.

After the war, as a reward for his rapid flight, Joe was flown in luxury from America to England. He brought his own pigeon food as a respect for rationing, and on arrival was met by an embassy car which took him to the Tower of London. There he was received by numerous officials including a British Major General who made a speech congratulating Joe personally, before placing the Dickin Medal round the pigeon's neck.

Not everyone, however, was convinced of a homing pigeon's ability to find its way. One soldier was ordered, as an exercise, to send two pigeons with important messages back to base. However, doubting the pigeons' sense of direction, he decided to take matters into his own hands. He reached headquarters some three and a half hours later – with the pigeons in a box, on his bicycle! When asked by an angry commanding officer what had happened to the messages, the exhausted soldier replied that he was worried the pigeons would not find their way on their own.

The value of homing pigeons during times of trouble cannot be stressed too highly. Many amazingly brave birds suffered immense dangers and physical injuries but still managed to complete their tasks, enabling important information to be passed on. Some birds were placed in cartons and dropped by parachute to the French Resistance, who used them to send back details of important concealed weapon launching installations. This enabled the RAF to see exactly where the targets were and to destroy such sites.

White Vision, a hen pigeon, was responsible for saving the lives of eleven men ditched in the sea when she flew sixty miles at an incredible speed over heavy seas and against a strong head wind. A search for the men had been abandoned due to bad weather but when White Vision's message was received, a further party was sent out and the men were recovered quickly and safely.

Royal Blue, a pigeon from the Sandringham Lofts, was

released from a crashed RAF plane in Holland and returned home with information about the crew in four hours, after flying 120 miles. Royal Blue was under one year old when he made his important flight and in 1945 a pigeon messenger was sent to Sandringham asking the King's permission to award Royal Blue the Dickin Medal. The King's acceptance message literally flew back to the Air Ministry and later Royal Blue proudly received his medal from Rear Admiral Roger Bellairs.

Two more birds recommended for Dickin Medals were Tyke and Winkie. In June 1943 Tyke carried an SOS message approximately 100 miles in poor visibility and the rescued men, an American air crew, said later that they owed their lives to his marvellous effort.

The crew of a Beaufort bomber forced into the North Sea also claimed that they owed their lives to their pigeon saviour. When the plane hit the water it broke up and Winkie managed to escape from her container. Although her wings were clogged with oil the bird flew 129 miles back to base and as a result a fresh search for the missing plane was mounted and all the crew rescued. Following their recovery, the men held a dinner for the pigeon at which she was guest of honour, and a small bronze plaque was inscribed to mark her gallant flight.

Some people may think that a homing pigeon's job is a fairly straightforward one, that by using their instincts they find their way home. In actual fact, birds vary in personality in much the same way that humans do. There are faint-hearted pigeons who give up at the first opportunity and abandon their mission, and there are fearless pigeons who overcome seemingly impossible odds in the execution of their task. There was even one account of a pigeon who sustained a broken wing during its flight, walking the last six miles back to its coop! If it were not for such feathered heroes, many more human lives would have been lost in the Wars and the Air Ministry Pigeon Section, realizing this, was quick to praise such brave efforts.

President Wilson was a battle-scarred bird who served during the First World War. In November 1918 he was released in France carrying an important message. He reached his destination some twenty-five miles away, after flying through fire and fog with the message hanging to a shattered leg and his body pierced by a bullet. President Wilson happily recovered and after the war was taken to the United States to enjoy a well earned rest at Fort Monmouth, where he died at eleven years of age.

Mary of Exeter served with the National Pigeon Service during the Second World War and won the Dickin Medal for her tremendous courage. She once suffered an attack from a hawk whilst on a mission and it was several days before she returned – still bearing her message – with her neck and breast ripped open. On another occasion, after disappearing for three weeks, she arrived back with three pellets in her body and part of a wing shot away. Later, during two bombing raids, Mary escaped whilst other pigeons in her loft were killed; and only a short time afterwards she was found almost dead in a field. Her owner nursed her carefully, feeding her by hand, until she regained some strength, but even then she had to wear a leather collar to support her head until her wounds were totally healed.

A pigeon, William of Orange, who proved to be exceptional under training, later distinguished himself at Arnhem when he was released carrying his message and flew the 260-mile distance over land and sea during bad weather conditions, in what was thought to be record time.

Another pigeon had a coded message registering the success of his mission broadcast on the BBC Dutch Service. In this case pigeon fancier and worker with the underground resistance movement in Holland, Mr Drijver, took care of an exhausted pigeon that he found lying in the road. Seeing that it bore an English ring, the man nursed it back to health, then he sent the bird back to England carrying a very valuable piece of military information. The pigeon also carried a request that if the message arrived safely it should be acknowledged in code over the radio, and delighted resistance workers later heard just what they were waiting for. In February 1946 Mr Drijver and Tommy the pigeon were guests of honour at a special celebration, where Tommy received his Dickin Medal from a Major General and Mr Drijver was presented with a pair of pedigree pigeons in recognition of his deed.

The first mission of a pigeon called Kenley Lass was one of extreme difficulty, for in 1940 she was dropped by parachute with an agent into enemy-occupied France. Following a nine-mile journey on foot, the pair then stayed in hiding for a further eleven days before the desired information could be obtained and Kenley Lass released to carry it back to England. Despite being confined for so long, the pigeon was soon safely back in her loft having covered an amazing 300 miles in one day.

Pigeon handlers needed to know their birds' temperaments so that they could be sure that the birds were able to deal with any situation that might arise. One man was asked to choose two birds for an important secret mission; the birds having to fly in the quickest possible time without being distracted. The man chose two females and introduced them separately to the same cock bird. The females were then set their task – which they completed in record time, returning only seconds apart to the waiting cock bird.

Two more pigeons, again Dickin Medal winners, were Paddy and Gustav, who came over from America to offer their services. Both pigeons gave excellent performances: Gustav being the first pigeon back to England from Normandy, and Paddy turning in the best recorded time during Normandy operations with the American Forces. The birds both brought their 'wives' with them; Gustav's wife Betty was also a valuable member of the pigeon force and when she was on a mission, Gustav took over the domestic routine of caring for the family. (When it comes to rearing offspring, pigeons are unique as they are the only birds to suckle their young, the milk forming in the crop of both male and female birds.) Paddy's wife, however, was more homely and although not active in flight operations she did play an important role, for Paddy was so fond of her that he always put in good flight times in his eagerness to get back to her.

Chapter Four

More Wartime Heroics

MASCOTS ARE STILL an important part of life in
the Forces today and during the war an animal
mascot often helped to boost morale amongst men fighting far
away from home. Trace horses, rescue dogs and police horses
were a regular feature of wartime years but many animals also
remained in civilian life and some of those managed to
demonstrate that they too could be a valuable help in times of
trouble.

One story concerned an Airedale bitch who, by her own
premonition, managed to save the lives of her owners. On the
night of an air raid, the dog's owners were sheltering under a
table in the basement of their home. The dog became
increasingly agitated and kept running to the cellar door and
back again. The man, his wife and their young son hesitated to
follow the dog, but the animal became insistent, whining and
trying to push them towards the coal cellar. At last the family
gave in to the dog's wishes and had only just got into the
cellar, when the whole house collapsed. The table under which
they had been sheltering was smashed to pieces and, had they
not taken refuge in the cellar, it is doubtful they would have
survived.

Sheila was the only dog who was not attached to the Forces,
to win the Dickin Medal. Hers was a 'reserved occupation' –
she was a working sheepdog. Sheila's territory was the
Cheviot Hills and in December 1944, during a blizzard, several
shepherds with their dogs set out to find a crashed American
aircraft. Sheila stayed beside her owner, Mr John Dagg, until
she reached the top of the hill. With visibility almost nil, the
dog disappeared into the snowstorm and shortly after managed
to find the airmen sheltering in a ravine. Sheila then guided
the rest of the party to the airmen and was subsequently

rewarded for her efforts. Mr Dagg was presented with the BEM for his part in the rescue and Sheila was made an honorary member of the Allied Forces Mascot Club, on recommendation from the Home Office, and awarded the Dickin Medal by Lady Rose. At the ceremony in her honour Sheila, realizing she could do no wrong, decided to lie on her back and wave her legs in the air, much to everyone's amusement.

This was not the end of Sheila's story, however, as the parents of one of the crewmen who lost his life in the crash became very interested in Mr Dagg and his Collie. They asked if they could have one of Sheila's puppies, and eventually permission was granted by the War Department in Washington. A beautiful bitch puppy was chosen and set off to make her home in South Carolina, so forging a special link between animal lovers of two countries.

Throughout the war, dogs continued to demonstrate that they could be man's best friend and during bombings they often proved they could be life-savers even when not a part of official rescue parties. Peggy was one such mongrel, who was awarded an inscribed collar by the RSPCA for her gallantry and courage.

Peggy lived at a house in East Anglia which was bombed, leaving her owner and family trapped under rubble. Peggy could have escaped through a window but she noticed that the baby in its pram was being suffocated by a fall of dust and plaster. Without hesitation, Peggy jumped on to the pram and, pawing furiously at the debris, made a hole big enough for the baby to breathe through. Then she sat down calmly to wait for rescuers, even though she sensed that at any moment a fresh fall of rubble could land on herself and the baby. Thankfully, mother, child and dog were all brought out safely and it was a tribute to Peggy's skill and patience that they all survived.

During the war many pets came to recognize the sound of the siren and took refuge with their owners in the family shelter.

One mongrel called Rex, who lived near Crystal Palace, decided that his appointed task, at the sound of the siren, was to ensure the safety of his owner and her neighbour. At the familiar sound, Rex would run into the hall and dislodge the gas mask from its place and then insist that his owner follow

him to the shelter. Any delay resulted in her being gently
pushed by her canine guardian. Rex then went back for her
next-door neighbour, and once both ladies were seated safely
in the shelter the dog would stand guard in the doorway,
keeping watch for the enemy. When danger had passed and
the 'All Clear' sounded, Rex accompanied the ladies back to
the house where he nonchalantly accepted their praise and
titbits for a job well done.

Slightly further afield, on the Isle of Man, a three-legged
hero distinguished himself. His name was Peg-leg, having lost
one leg as a puppy. One day he was out on the mountainside
when he found an unconscious airman. Apparently a plane
had crashed, killing some of the crew, but the radio operator,
despite severe wounds, had tried to crawl for help. Eventually,
close to death, he could go no further and it was then that the
dog appeared.

Peg-leg immediately knew that he had to get help and ran as
fast as he could back to his owners, Mr and Mrs Shooter.
Knowing Peg-leg to be a sensible dog, their suspicions were
aroused by his excited barks indicating a sense of urgency. Mrs
Shooter followed her dog as he led the way through a wood
and over a stream to where the injured man lay. Soon, thanks
to Peg-leg, the airman was on his way to hospital, his life
saved. In 1946 Peg-leg was nominated for a silver medal which
was presented to him before an important gathering of
dignitaries. However, the eleven-year-old dog found the
whole business rather tiring and slept contentedly for most of
the ceremony under his owner's chair.

When danger threatens, many animals forget their differ-
ences and live together quietly and amicably. This was
witnessed during bombing raids when, in one instance,
several streets were left in ruins. Different types of animals
found themselves homeless and, until arrangements could be
made for their welfare, they were collected and placed together
in one large room. During this time, rescue workers noticed
that not one fight broke out and cats and dogs lived together
quite peacefully.

Hardships prevailed for many people during the war and
were faced as stoically as possible, but some with pets found
themselves faced with difficult decisions to make when they
could no longer afford to feed their animals. One story was

told by a widow who, having a young son to support, found she could no longer keep their pet cat. Tearfully the woman told the cat that she would have to have her put to sleep the following day, due to the family's dire circumstances. The next day the cat was nowhere to be found, but eventually she returned with a dead wild rabbit she had killed. The cat continued to hunt for food, scarcely marking her prey, and always brought her contribution home, where she waited patiently for her share.

During the war, when human morale was often so low, an animal mascot frequently cheered up even the most dispirited. Judy, a Pointer bitch, was the mascot of several naval vessels and was an officially registered prisoner-of-war in the Far East. She was born in Shanghai in 1937 and presented to the Royal Navy. In 1942, whilst she was serving with HMS Grasshopper, the ship was attacked by Japanese aircraft and blown up. The crew, who had abandoned ship and were drifting in the lifeboats, eventually reached a small, uninhabited island, but they had only managed to salvage a little food and had no water. The men searched the island but could find no fresh drinking water and, feeling desperate, asked Judy to help. The dog walked along the shore, stopped and waited for two hours until the tide went out. Then she set off again, over the sand which had previously been covered by sea. Finally she stopped and started to drink from what turned out to be a fresh water spring. The crew were marooned for several days before being rescued, but unfortunately, following further events, dog and men were taken prisoner by the Japanese.

In a prison camp at Medan, Judy met Leading Aircraftman Frank Williams of the RAF. He shared his meagre rations of food with her and, as far as she was concerned, he became her master. Judy, besides boosting morale amongst the prisoners, gave the alarm whenever poisonous snakes, scorpions, alligators and even tigers were about. She had a family of nine pups and her hobby was chasing monkeys and flying foxes. On one occasion, to everyone's amusement, Judy found what must surely be every dog's dream – an elephant bone. There was one drawback however: it took her nearly two hours to bury it!

When the prisoners were to be shipped to Singapore, Judy was sentenced to remain behind. However, Frank Williams hid her in a sack and told her not to make a sound. For three hours Judy lay in the sack in the scorching sun. The guards were very suspicious but Judy kept quiet and still, never even whimpering throughout her ordeal.

After further escapades, Judy and her fellow prisoners were released. She was awarded the Dickin Medal on her return to England, and her bark was heard by thousands of people listening to the BBC programmes which were a feature of Britain's victory celebrations.

A mongrel called Daisy was the mascot of a Norwegian trawler which was hit by a torpedo, throwing the crew into an icy sea. Some were killed outright but those who survived faced a long, cold wait to be rescued. Daisy, sensing the men's desperately low morale, spent all night swimming from one to another, licking their faces as if to encourage them to hang on. At last the crew were safely picked up and taken to Britain where every man claimed that Daisy had given him comfort and hope during the long, cold, dark hours.

In recognition of her courage and devotion, Daisy was awarded a presentation collar inscribed with the words 'For Valour' by the RSPCA. Daisy was then given a new job as mascot of a Norwegian Seamen's Hostel in Newcastle, where she settled happily, and became the proud mother of two pups. People were so interested in her story that they would call into the RSPCA headquarters to ask how she was getting on and whether she had gone to sea again.

Many animals who served their country had no choice but to do so, although occasionally some seemed to relish a life of excitement and danger. Certainly this was the case with one famous soldier serving in Northern Ireland. He was attached to the Grenadier Guards, the Marines, The Queen's Own Highlanders and the Welsh Guards and did a tremendous job of boosting morale. He was, of course, Rats the mongrel, much loved by members of the British Army units in Crossmaglen. He was a very affectionate animal and quickly became a favourite with the men, accompanying them on patrols and car chases. He suffered gun shot wounds and even had part of his tail burnt off by a fire bomb. Rats had various pieces of metal lodged in his body and managed, on two occasions, to get himself run over by cars which left his paws permanently bent. His special trick was to leap from a helicopter as it was coming in to land – sometimes jumping 30 feet to the ground! As reports of his exploits spread, Rats became a national celebrity and appeared on television – eventually needing a staff of six soldiers to answer the two sacks of fan mail he received each day. In 1980, for health reasons, Rats was honorably retired at a special ceremony and the much loved soldier went to live peacefully in Kent.

Further afield, in South Africa, a Great Dane called Just Nuisance became a legend in his own lifetime and his statue in Simonstown has become a popular collection point for animal welfare groups in the Cape Peninsula. In his short seven years of life, the dog raised money for wartime naval charities and even saved a man's life, besides getting involved in various notable escapades. He also became the only member of the Royal Navy, from an Ordinary Seaman to Admiral of the Fleet, to be excused by Admiralty Orders from wearing a cap.

Nuisance becarr.e famous for his attachment to the sailors who frequented the United Services Institute in Simonstown, where the dog lived with his owner Mr Chaney. He developed a preference for seamen in 'square rig' uniform, i.e. bell-bottomed trousers, and rapidly became known as a 'ratings' dog. As Nuisance was so often seen in the company of sailors, it was decided that he should be enlisted in the Royal Navy and so, on 25 August 1939, he was officially given the rank of Able Seaman; his registration documents declaring his occupation to be 'Bonecrusher'.

The dog's parents were both pedigree Great Danes and as Nuisance was born at Rondebosch, a Cape Town suburb, his title at the S.A. Kennel Union was 'Pride of Rondebosch'. He acquired the name of Just Nuisance as a result of sunning himself on the deck of a cruiser moored at Simonstown. The Great Dane had a habit of lying full length on one of the most frequently used gangways so that members of the crew found themselves having to step over his body, much to their annoyance, as they went about their duties. However, as the dog measured just under two metres (standing upright on his hind legs) and weighed 67 kg, no one was prepared to argue with him!

Stories of Nuisance's adventures, including being kidnapped on one occasion, began to spread and he seemed to make news wherever he went. Although he was highly thought of by many, he was no saint, as his naval 'conduct sheets' revealed: 'Character – very good, Efficiency – moderate, Discipline – poor'. Certain instances of misconduct included going AWOL, sleeping on other sailor's beds without permission and refusing to leave pubs at closing time after sailor friends had been buying him his favourite drink – lager.

Nuisance did have some redeeming qualities however, such as standing to attention every time the British National Anthem was played, and escorting sailors back to base after they had spent a night 'on the town'. The Great Dane proved he could be a marvellous ally not only to the sailors but to a Bulldog called Ajax, whom he befriended. On occasions when a larger dog was pestering Ajax, Nuisance would come bounding up; one bark from him was enough to scare other dogs away. Another time the two dogs had been playing on the beach when Ajax started to limp after stepping on a spiny sea creature. Nuisance was immediately concerned for his friend and made Ajax walk up and down in the sea water for about an hour until he was satisfied that the Bulldog's limp was cured.

Nuisance was equally anxious when sailors started fighting and the huge dog would intervene by standing on his hind legs and pushing the men apart with his paws. Then, once they were separated, he would stalk between them growling.

At the shore based naval establishment where Nuisance was stationed, he also warned others of snakes and scorpions and on at least two occasions killed both, but it was by saving a man's life that Nuisance received most acclaim. Standing beside the perimeter fence at the camp base was an isolated toilet used mostly by sentry patrols on duty during the night. One evening as a transport vehicle passed some distance away, the driver saw Nuisance barking in the doorway, and decided to investigate. The dog led the way to a man lying unconscious on the floor and refused to leave him until an ambulance arrived. The man was later diagnosed as having a severe case of malaria and without medical attention would soon have died.

Nuisance was hailed as a hero and as a reward for his actions he was given fourteen days leave and double rations of meat and bones. He had become such a celebrity that news of his exploits helped to boost the morale of visiting sailors during the war. He was held in such high esteem that there was great concern when he became ill and was found to have developed a crippling paralysis. He was eventually put to sleep on 1 April 1944 and buried with full naval honours at Klaver Camp near Simon's Town. Buglers sounded the Last Post and more than a hundred sailors came to say goodbye to a dearly loved friend.

Men of the Coldstream Guards had a rather unusual hero – Jacob the goose. A battalion of the Coldstream Guards was stationed near Quebec in October 1838. One day the guardsman on sentry duty saw a large goose waddling about and feeding close by. Suddenly a fox appeared and the goose froze. The guardsman could not fire his musket to scare away the fox for fear of alerting the whole battalion who would think they were being attacked by rebels, who were rumoured to be nearby. The goose came to life, started racing about madly, shrieking in wild panic, and suddenly darted towards the man and stuck its head between his legs. The fox gave chase but was soon thwarted by the guardsman's bayonet and the relieved goose rubbed its head against the sentry's legs in grateful thanks for saving its life. That night the goose went back to its home – a neighbouring farm – but every morning from then on it returned to the sentry post and accompanied successive guardsmen on sentry duty. Two months later the goose, now christened Jacob, was to save the life of the guardsman who had originally rescued it from the fox.

One cold November night Jacob did not return to the farm as usual but remained with the sentry. The goose seemed uneasy and kept peering towards the direction of the farm when suddenly, under cover of darkness, rebels charged at the guardsman with knives drawn. The goose rushed at the attackers with flapping wings and loud cries, giving the sentry a chance to fire a shot and rouse the others, who drove off the intruders. When the commanding officer heard of Jacob's bravery, he bought the goose from the farmer and as a reward, the officers presented Jacob with a golden collar which he wore whilst strutting around the barracks. When the guards returned to England, Jacob went too, continuing his sentry duties to the delight of the crowds who came to see him. The goose was a firm favourite with children who brought him titbits, and he even came to the attention of the Duke of Wellington who was said to have admired Jacob's devotion to duty.

Another rather unusual animal became a mascot when Albert Marr's pet accompanied him to his South African regiment in the First World War. The baboon, called Jackie, was soon a firm favourite with the men, who found him so friendly and intelligent that he was given the role of regimental mascot, together with his own rations and uniform. Jackie's excellent hearing enabled him to warn the men of an enemy approach, which he did by giving a little bark or tugging at his owner's uniform. When Albert Marr was hit by a bullet, Jackie refused to leave his side until help arrived. In 1918 one of Jackie's legs had to be amputated due to a severe shrapnel wound but despite fears for his life, the baboon made a full recovery and was promoted to the rank of corporal. After the war Jackie was presented with a medal and took part in the Lord Mayor's victory parade through London, sitting proudly on top of a captured German howitzer.

Another mascot called Donald – what else but a duck? – lived for about eighteen months as a prisoner-of-war in Thailand, and boosted morale amongst the captured men of the 2nd Gordon Highlanders. It seemed that Donald's days were numbered when orders were received that all pets were to be destroyed, however one soldier came to the duck's rescue by informing the guards that Donald was a sacred bird. William Gray told his captors that ducks were held in high esteem by the Scots and that Donald was worshipped by the prisoners every morning. Suitably impressed with this tale, the Japanese guards agreed to let the men keep Donald (who was, incidentally, female). In the months that followed, Donald laid some 160 eggs which were distributed amongst the sick prisoners and in 1945 she returned with William Gray to Aberdeenshire where she spent her days in peaceful retirement.

Horses played an important role during the war in many ways. The calmness displayed by police horses in particular was a great help in setting a good example to others. On some occasions when a milk pony or van horse seemed terrified, an officer would bring his horse alongside and this had the effect of reassuring the panicked animal. Police horses also had to walk over jagged metal, broken glass and nails which littered the streets after a raid, but the brave animals suffered such hazards time and again with fortitude.

An amazing sixth sense operates in horses as well as dogs,

and this was illustrated by a police horse called Ubique. The bay gelding was on patrol one day during flying bomb attacks when, as he was entering a main road from a side turning, he stopped in his tracks and completely refused to move on. His rider, PC L. Salmon, was surprised but did not try to force him, and only a few seconds later a flying bomb hit the main road in exactly the spot they would have reached had they gone straight on.

Two horses, Quetta and Regal, displayed tremendous courage when they were covered in debris during raids in which their stables were hit. PC J. Brady was standing in the stall beside bay mare Quetta, when a flying bomb exploded nearby. The man only had time to fling himself to the ground as the windows crashed and the black-out was blown inside. All the other horses moved about restlessly but when PC Brady looked up he saw Quetta standing quietly beside him, covered in debris and with broken glass all around her. Although she had been startled, she had been careful not to touch the man lying almost under her hooves.

Regal certainly lived up to his name. When bombs caused fire to break out in a nearby building, flames soon spread to the stables. Regal showed no sign of panic as danger threatened, and when at last help arrived he allowed himself to be led quietly to safety. Regal's composure enabled his rescuers to complete their task quickly and effectively. Some three years later a bomb fell within yards of the same building, this time covering the horse in rubble and giving him some injuries from the flying fragments. However, as before, Regal remained calm, and later he received an award for his bravery and self control.

'Our Dumb Friends' League', a society aimed at encouraging kindness to animals, was formed in 1897, and in 1906 it opened the first Animals' Hospital to provide treatment for animals of needy owners. This hospital never closed its doors throughout two world wars and in spite of being bombed, remained open both day and night. The society later joined with the Blue Cross to become 'The Blue Cross (incorporating Our Dumb Friends' League)'. The Blue Cross had started in 1912 and became well-known in the First World War when its symbol was flown over the horse hospitals, distinguishing them from the Red Cross troop hospitals.

The Trace Horse Scheme was started in 1905 by Our Dumb Friends' League, whereby draught horses used their enormous strength to give assistance to others in need. A draught horse would be stationed at the foot of a particular hill, and with the aid of connecting traces (or straps) the large horse would help smaller horses to pull the heavily laden carts to the top of the hill. At one time there were over a dozen hills being worked in the London area, in places such as Haverstock Hill, Wimbledon Hill, Kingston Hill and Church Street, Kensington. Many large firms used the horses, paying for their 'pull up' the hill, whilst poor owners were given the assistance free. The Trace Horse attendant was given instructions that he should never refuse to help but that he was to report any cases of deliberate over-loading.

'Wimbledon Jack' was probably the most well-known Trace Horse and when he died in 1939 the scheme closed. In one six-month period he made 1,803 trips up the particularly long, steep Wimbledon Hill. Before Jack several other horses had been tried but none were really found to be strong enough. Tommy and Ginger were two other Trace Horses who worked at Kingston Hill and Haverstock Hill, respectively. Many smaller horses were grateful for the invaluable assistance these animals gave, as fodder rations depleted the horses' strength so that journeys became that much harder than usual. Also, many road surfaces had suffered the effects of the war, making the ascent of hills even more taxing.

Two horses who performed their duties admirably during the war, were Olga and Upstart. They were based with the Mounted Branch of the Metropolitan Police Force and won Dickin Medals for their courage in carrying out duties. Olga, a bay mare, was out on patrol in London in 1944 when a flying bomb exploded near her. The horse felt the effects of the blast which destroyed four houses and caused extensive damage to other buildings. Just as her rider PC Thwaites was attempting to steady her, a plate-glass window shattered and crashed into the road immediately in front of her. This was too much for Olga who bolted, but who was calmed once again by her rider and persuaded to return to the scene. There Olga remained standing quietly, so that her rider was able to assist rescue parties by excluding sightseers and controlling traffic.

Upstart was a handsome chestnut gelding based at Hyde

Park. His stables were twice damaged by enemy action but Upstart coped well with the noise and chaos. One day, when he was being ridden by District Inspector Morley in the Bethnal Green area of London, a flying bomb exploded 75 yards away, showering them both with metal and broken glass. Again, help was needed to assist the rescue operations, so Upstart remained on duty, setting a fine example of courage and steadfastness.

The men who are picked for the Mounted Branch, work as much as possible with one horse for the whole of their career. The horse and its chosen rider are introduced to each other at Imber Court, the training centre of the Mounted Police Branch, and often the men become so close to their horses that they do not like to go on leave because it means being parted from them. During training the horses learn to cope with crowds, bands and gun shots, but in wartime they also had to get used to bombs, mines, rockets and the wail of sirens.

At the start of the war, as an experiment, each horse was given extra feed at the sound of the alert. The theory was that the horse would connect the sound with something pleasant. However, as the horses started to get fat it was decided that the idea should be abandoned. Unfortunately the horses did not approve of this new ruling and uproar broke out when the sirens sounded and no food was produced.

During the First World War, dogs were used to find wounded soldiers on the battlefield during a lull in the fighting and in the Second World War rescue dogs were a common sight, particularly around London. Two animals who helped to pioneer rescue work were Rip and Beauty. Before dogs were officially trained to trace casualties, the people involved in finding victims amongst the debris had a long and arduous task, often having to guess where to start digging.

Mongrel Rip was found homeless and starving after a raid in 1940. He became the mascot of the Southill Street ARP in Poplar, East London, and during heavy gunfire and bombing raids Rip was always on duty, never getting in the way but working quickly to sniff out casualties. He had over five years active service to his credit and received his Dickin Medal in 1945, as did Beauty.

Tipperary Beauty, to give the dog her full name, was a wirehaired Terrier belonging to Mr Barnet, a superintendent of the PDSA and leader of a rescue squad. Beauty used to accompany the rescue party in their searches amongst the ruins of East London and it was on her own initiative that she started lifesaving. A total of sixty-three animals were rescued through her efforts and she was often seen digging so hard that her paws bled: so admirers gave her some leather boots to wear. She was presented with the PDSA Pioneer Medal (normally only given to humans), the Dickin Medal and also given 'the freedom of Holland Park and all the trees therein'.

Another famous dog was Rex, whose story has appeared on a children's television programme. Rex was a black and tan German Shepherd who started out as a guard dog but had such a gentle disposition that he was sent to work with the rescue parties instead. Rex worked in the East End of London, near the docks, and rescued other dogs and cats as well as people. It was Rex's job to alert the civil defence workers who then dug out the victims. On one occasion when he was already suffering the effects of gas, he repeatedly entered a burning building and succeeded in rescuing ten people. He saved a total of sixty-three lives during similar operations and once worked for ten hours without a rest.

In the course of duty, Rex and other rescue dogs often suffered bomb blasts, gas fumes and burnt paws but all continued to work with amazing dedication. At the end of the war Rex, who was then still only two years old, was awarded the Dickin Medal for bravery – a fitting tribute to a very special dog. He went on to raise hundreds of pounds for the People's Dispensary for Sick Animals and in 1985 the Imperial War Museum arranged an exhibition in his honour.

Irma, a beautiful German Shepherd rescue dog, always seemed to know whether a casualty trapped under rubble was alive or not. If the person was alive, Irma would bark happily but if he was dead, she would simply wag her tail to indicate his presence underground, and when dead bodies were brought out, Irma would lick their faces and look at her handler earnestly as if begging him to bring them back to life.

On one occasion, when the rescuers were convinced they had recovered everyone from a destroyed building, Irma insisted that they continue their search and refused to leave a certain spot. Although sceptical, the workers carried on digging and at last two small girls were discovered, both alive.

On another occasion Irma was working with a companion called Psyche. Both dogs ran to the same place in the rubble and indicated a victim. The debris concealed a woman who had been trapped for nine hours beneath two collapsed floors. Rescue workers had not suspected the woman's presence and had been walking over the exact spot where she was buried.

Anyone doubting an animal's sixth sense must have wondered at Irma's instincts. Once, when a victim was dug out, Irma started barking repeatedly although the person appeared to be quite dead. Later the victim regained consciousness and Irma was once again proved right. Irma proudly took part in the victory celebration march in 1946 and even met the Queen. Irma's companion that day was another rescue dog called Peter, who delighted crowds by answering their applause with excited barks. The dogs were congratulated and praised by the Queen but the honour of meeting royalty was lost on Peter – he was more interested in the Queen's fur wrap!

Another dog taking part in the victory celebrations was Jet, a handsome black dog who had already served a distinguished career in anti-sabotage work before joining the rescue services. Jet was not a very good traveller and once arrived in London after a 100-mile journey during which he had been very sick. After only a brief rest his help was requested at a London suburb where a person was missing. Jet soon located the victim just as he did on another occasion when he found a hundred and twenty-five people trapped under a pile of rubble, after a Chelsea block of flats had been hit by a flying bomb. Jet, like numerous other dogs, was continually in action until the end of the war and many people undoubtedly owed their lives to him and his colleagues.

Some rescue stories had rather unusual endings. For example, one handler and his dog were busy searching a spot in a ruin which the dog had indicated. As they tunnelled through the debris the pair could hear a voice swearing. The handler immediately called for an ambulance and reassured the victim that help was on its way. Further digging continued until a smashed cage was discovered, containing a loudly cursing and very cross parrot!

The dogs were obviously highly thought of by the people they rescued, but they had a special place in the hearts of their

handlers also. After the war the dogs were returned to their
original owners, to the heartbreak of their handlers with whom
they had worked so well. One handler said of 'his' dog later:
'Do I miss him? Every day I think of him. He was a pal any
man could be proud of. In fun, in fear, in danger he was
always beside me and always ready to help mankind. What
more could one ask of any animal?'[†]

[†]This is a quote from Mr. W. Rowe and appears in the book *They Also Serve – A
History of the PDSA* by Dorothea St. Hill Bourne.

Chapter Five

A Job to Do

MANY DOGS these days assist the authorities with their work, but not so long ago there was a call to replace German drug-sniffing police dogs with pigs!

Werner Franke, a dog handler with the German Police Force, decided to experiment by using a pig in drug detection, reasoning that pigs have lots of energy, are intelligent and have a highly developed sense of smell. After all, they have been successfully used for generations to sniff out that much prized delicacy, truffles. He picked Luise, born on 7 July 1984, and soon found her very sociable and unafraid of anything. Werner started by making up small bags filled with drugs and every time Luise touched one with her nose, she was given a reward. Soon, she was able to detect drugs and explosives buried 70 centimetres underground.

Unfortunately, because of her size and weight, Luise was not allowed to live with her handler, so she shared her kennel with a police watchdog, a Rottweiler called Bill, of whom she became very fond. At one time the 200-pound pig was suspended from her job after fears that she was bad for the police image. Fortunately, following intervention by the Greens Party in Lower Saxony and countless letters of protest, Luise was reprieved.

Her excellent sniffing abilities meant that she was often beating the Force's top German Shepherd dogs during training sessions, but the Ministry rejected a plea for all police dogs to be replaced with pigs. The media in Europe, America and Canada became interested in her story and Luise found herself the centre of attention; she visited Berlin on a goodwill tour and even appeared on the stage of the Hanover Opera – in a non-vocal role – during a special Christmas performance.

Dogs, however, still remain firm favourites for drug detection with police forces all over the world, and in America one dog found herself on an underworld 'hit list' after she discovered $250,000 worth of drugs – subsequently leading to over twenty-five major arrests. For her own protection the police dog now stays at a different place every night and her handler, ever-vigilant for would-be assassins, personally prepares all the dog's meals.

One famous animal who made the Guinness Book of Records for his drug-sniffing abilities, was a Golden Retriever called Intrepid (or Trep for short). The dog located drugs on a boat which had previously been searched four times by the authorities, and Trep apparently made legal history when he was issued with his own search warrant. One story has it that during a demonstration exercise at a school, when Trep was supposed to find ten hidden packets of drugs, he found eleven! No one could deny Trep's devotion to duty.

Another dog, Oscar, a pedigree English Springer Spaniel, became an overnight celebrity when he was chosen to give a demonstration of drug detection in front of the Princess of Wales. The drugs were hidden in a suitcase and Oscar soon alerted everyone to the fact. Indeed, such was his enthusiasm that he would not let go of the case, much to the amusement of the Princess, who was clearly impressed by his absolute dedication! Following the display, Oscar made a TV appearance, and as a result numerous offers were made of suitable mating partners for the dog, plus considerable amounts of money for his services at stud. (Customs & Excise did not allow Oscar to take up these opportunities and the dog's views on the subject will never be known!) Due to Oscar's diligence at work, there are several drug smugglers now serving prison sentences who would probably be surprised to discover that their fate was a result of the efforts of a Springer Spaniel.

The dogs used by H.M. Customs & Excise are all trained by the Royal Air Force Dog School whose motto is: 'Trained to perfection – with kindness'. The training centre at RAF Newton in Nottingham accepts dogs donated by the public, such as Gun dog breeds (Border Collies, Labradors, Retrievers, etc.) of both sexes and also German Shepherd dogs (not bitches). Approximately 1,300 animals are offered annually although only some 60 per cent are eventually accepted into the Air Force. Once they have completed their training, the dogs are able to detect various drugs, all cleverly disguised. It is a fallacy that the dogs only work because they are addicted to drugs. Quite simply, the dogs enjoy it – to them it is merely a game.

At the turn of the century, thousands of ponies worked in the coal mines and although the number has gradually declined, a tribute must be paid to their excellent work – and on occasions, their life-saving intuition. In 1842 the Mine Act banned women, girls and boys under ten years of age from working in the pits, and ponies were brought in to undertake the haulage work in their place. In 1914 there were approximately 70,000 horses being used, but since then the numbers have gradually declined due to mechanization and there are only about forty still working in Britain today.

Although machines have taken over much of the underground work, the ponies still have jobs to do, frequently hauling the component parts of the conveyors that will eventually replace the four-legged workers. One old myth regarding the animals was that all pit ponies were blind. This belief may have been due to the special blinkers which were part of the harness and designed to protect the ponies' eyes – no blind pony was allowed to work in the mine under any circumstances.

Some pits with thick coal seams employed horses, but the majority of mines found ponies more suitable – particularly small Shetland ponies who could negotiate the very low seams and narrow passages. All the animals were geldings – mares were not used in case of possible disruptions – and since the 1911 Coal Mines Act the ponies' welfare has been carefully monitored. For example, they must never be ridden and their working week is limited to forty-eight hours. Every pony has to have a complete medical check-up by a vet at least once a year and a written report must be carried out every day detailing the pony's condition. Care and attention is also paid to the ponies' living quarters; the design and equipment of stables is strictly defined and under today's law limewashing of the walls must be carried out at least every three months.

The ponies have to be a minimum of four years old and have undergone several weeks of training before they are allowed to go down a mine. They quickly learn to back up to a tub and

stand still whilst the wooden limbers (portable shafts connecting the harness to the tub) are positioned, and most animals
know without looking how many tubs are attached. A two-tub
pony will refuse to move if three tubs are attached and will
only proceed when one tub has been taken off.

Besides being companions and assistants to the mine
workers, there have also been instances when ponies have
saved mens' lives – either by refusing to move when they
sensed danger or even by grabbing a miner's shirt in their teeth
to prevent them going on. In some cases the roof has collapsed
minutes later.

A handsome chestnut called Ben gave one such warning and
saved his young 'driver's' life. Ben's driver had a habit of
sharing his sandwiches with his pony but on one occasion Ben
stayed some distance away, refusing all enticements. Instead
he kept pawing the ground and shaking his head. As his driver
appeared to be taking no notice, Ben's uneasiness increased
and he started prancing in a circle, whinnying loudly, then
backing away a few paces. The driver gradually became
worried by Ben's strange behaviour and eventually decided to
follow the agitated pony. Moments after he had done so, the
roof caved in and the sandwich box which he had been holding
seconds earlier was crushed under rock.

During the 1930s pit ponies became popular attractions at
county shows with the result that many people offered to
adopt the animals as they retired. Although letters are still
received by the Coal Board asking for ponies, those animals
currently working already have arrangements made for them
with carefully vetted homes, where they will be assured of a
happy and carefree retirement.

The oldest pit pony was reputed to be a skewbald called Ant
who worked for twenty-four years at a colliery in Gwent,
Wales. It was estimated that during his service down the mine
he travelled somewhere in the region of 70,000 miles. When
Ant's working life came to an end, he was adopted by a retired
miner, Mr Davies, who ran a small pub with the added bonus
of an adjoining field. Ant quickly attracted a fan club and the
local schoolchildren adopted him as a pet. When Mr Davies
died, his daughter took over Ant's welfare and used to give
him three meals a day plus a pint of stout after each meal as a
treat. Ant had become such a celebrity that when he died BBC

Wales broadcast the news, resulting in numerous floral tributes and hand-drawn cards of sympathy from children.

The use of birds to detect poisonous gas (i.e. carbon monoxide) in mines is still required by law today. Initially, trials also involving mice were carried out but the mice were found to be rather unreliable and eventually canaries and linnets were employed. Apparently, it was also discovered that a light-coloured bird was more sensitive to gas than a dark one. Although changes in the law are imminent, existing legislation requires every mine to keep two small birds, even though instruments are also used to give more accurate readings.

Some twelve birds would normally be kept at a Mine Rescue Station and two birds per mine are housed in aviaries on the surface. An employee – usually a bird fancier – undertakes to look after the canaries, some of which are bred by British Coal, whilst others are purchased from local breeders. If a bird is taken underground it would be used for eight hours or less, depending on the circumstances, and there is no doubt that the men become very attached to the tiny songsters, and take great care of them.

The birds are valuable 'rescue workers' when parties are exploring suspected gas in a mine, since they are more quickly affected by noxious fumes than the men, and so give an early warning of danger. The first indication is that the bird becomes less lively, but the canary is quickly revived by use of its own oxygen supply bottle attached to the cage.

Sheepdogs are another example of animals sharing men's lives and helping everyday work to run smoothly. These dogs regard their duties as looking after and herding their flock; a job they take very seriously as Mr Priestly of Hathersage Farm found out.

Some sheep had been grazing on a moor when they fell about 30 feet down a gully and were stranded on a rocky ledge about a foot wide. Below the ledge was a sheer drop of 70 feet. Eventually the sheep were located and a rescue plan was devised. Mr Priestly and his friend Mr Stone were lowered on to the ledge by ropes, as were the dogs Jaff and Moss.

The two black and white Border Collies were placed on guard to stop the sheep jumping and then the men roped each sheep in turn so that it could be pulled to safety. Mr Priestly then tried to rope his dogs so that they could be hauled up, but the animals refused to obey his orders. As far as they were concerned, they were not leaving whilst their master was still in danger. It was only when Mr Priestly had reached safety that the dogs allowed themselves to be pulled up. Jaff and Moss were bred by Mr Priestly who was devoted to them and he was delighted when they received silver medals from the PDSA at a special ceremony in London.

Mention mountain rescue avalanche work and most people immediately think of one type of dog – the St. Bernard – trudging through the snow to rescue unfortunate travellers. The Great St. Bernard Pass was used by travellers as far back as 800 BC and during winter months snowdrifts could average 65 feet deep whilst temperatures dropped as low as 20°F below zero. St. Bernard de Menthon founded a hospice in 1049 and the dogs were originally brought in to serve as guards. However, the animals soon began to accompany the monks on their rescue missions and by the 18th century were being used to find travellers lost or trapped in the snow. (St. Bernards did not actually carry barrels of brandy around their necks, but nevertheless managed to save numerous lives.)

In 1856 the hospice kennels were hit by an avalanche which, together with an outbreak of distemper, almost wiped out the breed which were descended from the Molossian dogs of ancient Greece and Rome. Due to the dire circumstances, the monks decided to introduce breeds of Great Dane, Newfoundland and Great Pyrenees in an effort to save their remaining dogs from extinction and to restore some strength and stamina to the stock.

Only smooth coated dogs were kept at the hospice as long fur quickly became clogged with snow, making movement difficult for the animal. Those dogs with a heavier rough-coat were given homes by Swiss fanciers down in the valleys and the St. Bernard that is known today was bred from this line. Because they looked like bears, people originally called them 'barihunds', but the dogs were officially named St. Bernard in 1862 at a show in England.

One famous St. Bernard, Barry, was born around 1800 and trained in the Swiss Alps. He was an excellent example of his breed and saved more than forty people during his lifetime. A tireless worker, Barry quickly forged a path through the snow, with his huge paws and chest, when he sensed someone was in danger. If he was then unable to help the victim, he would race back to the monastery and summon assistance with his actions and barks.

Barry's fame soon spread and there were many tales of his exploits. One such story describes how he saved the life of a child by carrying the youngster to safety on his back. On another occasion, legend has it that Barry was injured by the man he had just rescued. The man thought that the enormous dog was attacking him and tried to fight him off with a knife.

Barry retired from duties in 1812 and spent the rest of his days peacefully. He died in 1814 and later his body was preserved and placed on display at the Natural History Museum in Berne. In order to honour his memory, the name 'Barry' was reserved for only the most outstanding dogs at the hospice. St. Bernards can be found at the monastery to this day, proving a great attraction with visitors. They are also a constant reminder that more than 2,000 people, over the years, have owed their lives to these canine heroes.

The Search And Rescue Dog Association in Britain was formed in 1965 as a result of the marvellous impression the Swiss rescue dogs made on Hamish MacInnes of the Glencoe Mountain Rescue Team. After a visit to Switzerland he organized a pilot training course in Scotland for six dogs and handlers, realizing that the dogs could be trained to work both in summer and winter conditions.

SARDA's dogs are hand-picked for their speed and intelligence and need to be capable of maintaining an interest in their work for long periods, over difficult mountainous terrain. The rescue dogs must also possess exceptional scenting abilities and be large enough to tackle deep snow conditions. For these reasons German Shepherds, Labradors and Collies are the most popular breeds.

At first, for the novice dog, the search is merely a game of hide-and-seek, but SARDA trains its dogs meticulously; they must be obedient and all must pass the 'livestock test'. This means that when the handler walks towards sheep, causing them to run, the dog must be completely under control and must not chase or worry the flock in any way. If a dog fails this test, it is immediately withdrawn from the course.

The dog and handler teams are examined during training by

a panel of assessors. The dogs undergo rigorous tests which include jumping into helicopters, whilst the handlers must be competent rock climbers and possess a good working knowledge of first aid and navigation. Once trained, the dogs are re-tested at least every three years.

SARDA dogs are now widely used throughout Britain and in avalanche conditions 'the dogs have proved to be 50 per cent faster than any other known method of search'.[†] This can sometimes mean an early end to the work so that rescuers are not kept at prolonged risk. It is reckoned that a fully trained dog is worth twenty human searchers, but it is imperative that the dogs are called out early – not left as a last resort. SARDA dogs track by scent and some dogs can pick up an air-borne scent at nearly a mile from its source – even water does not deter these animals.

Each dog has only one handler and cannot be used by anyone else in the rescue team. Needless to say, these canine heroes are invaluable when searching in bad visibility or at night, and they wear bright scarlet jackets with a small light attached, so that the handlers can spot them and redirect them if necessary. The rescue dogs are capable of finding people buried under as much as four feet of snow and they indicate their 'find' by barking. They also serve another purpose if the victim is suffering from exposure, as a dog's higher-than-human body temperature makes it an ideal hot-water bottle!

One dog, a black Labrador called Jet, was part of a team which helped to find over thirty people lost on Welsh mountains, and in 1983 he was honoured by the PRO-Dogs charity when he received their 'Devotion to Duty' medal. Another dog, called Spruce, showed her extraordinary resilience after an accidental fall of 40 feet into a quarry. Although suffering from concussion, she was back at work within weeks.

The human rescuers are often in danger too. One handler and his dog were searching near a summit in the Cairngorms when winds gusted up to 100 m.p.h. Other SARDA members have worked with their dogs during 'white-outs' – having to throw snowballs ahead to find the edge of a ridge. (They only knew the path was still there when they saw the snowballs smash.)

[†]This is a quote from the SARDA (Scottish Highlands) leaflet *History of the Rescue Dogs*.

The abilities of rescue dogs puts them in demand during natural disasters, such as when an earthquake hit El Salvador, and David Jones, a SARDA member in Wales, and his Collie Meg were sent by the Association to the stricken area.

SARDA's unpaid volunteers are bound by an unwritten law never to refuse a call for help, and anyone can summon a rescue team simply by contacting the local police. Still a relatively young organization, SARDA aims to continue its charity-dependent work and maintain a valuable service that is free of charge.

What is believed to be the first overseas award given by the RSPCA was presented to Lorna, a police dog working in Hong Kong. Lorna was instructed to give chase when a man, suspected by the police, was seen outside a factory one morning. Lorna cornered the man, but instead of surrendering, he produced an axe and attacked the dog, wounding her in the face. Lorna refused to give up and held on to the suspect who was eventually arrested and convicted of burglary. Lorna received every possible care and attention, and was fully recovered when she collected her award from the RSPCA, at a special ceremony.

Another dog who was convalescing from injuries received biscuits, chocolates and even teddy bears from school children wishing him a speedy recovery. Rebel was brought in to help two police officers when they were threatened by a man they were trying to arrest. However the man, wielding a machete, repeatedly attacked Rebel, almost blinding him. The dog had to be carried to a police van by his handler, PC Devine, who held Rebel in his arms during an emergency dash to the vet. A ninety-minute operation saved the dog's life and incredibly, within three weeks, Rebel was back on patrol. His remarkable recovery may have had something to do with all the letters, drawings and cards (plus countless presents) he received from his fans. When he was well enough, Rebel sent a letter of thanks to the school children (written on his behalf by PC Devine) and even appeared on television. But like all hard-working police dogs he did not let the fame go to his head – he just took all the fuss in his stride. It is a case of 'duty first'.

The working animals and their handlers mentioned in this chapter are just a few of the many hundreds of 'unsung heroes'. Many do receive awards in recognition of their services and in the case of PC Bratchell and his dog Khan, no one could deny that they both thoroughly deserved them.

Khan and PC Bratchell were attempting to stop two men suspected of criminal damage, when the men tried to escape. They were ordered to halt but refused to do so and Khan was instructed to chase and detain them. The dog set off in hot pursuit, but suddenly he was hit by a passing car and trapped underneath it. When PC Bratchell reached the scene, he somehow managed to lift the car high enough for Khan to free himself. The dog wasted no time in continuing the chase and eventually managed to stop the men by circling and barking in the 'stand off' position.

Once the men were arrested, Khan collapsed from his injuries and had to be rushed to a vet. Following emergency treatment, Khan made a full recovery and was soon back on duty. PC Bratchell received an RSPCA Certificate of Merit for lifting the car off Khan, and the brave dog received the Society's Plaque for Intelligence and Courage, for the way in which he carried out his orders despite severe injuries.

It seems amazing that these animals should still be willing to work after facing such ordeals but it is undoubtedly their dedication to duty, plus the care and patience of their handlers which inspires them to continue.

Dogs are not the only ones who can help the police, however. One line of valuable information came from a rather unusual source when a shop in Israel was broken into. Unknown to the thieves, a parrot was listening to their conversation and later dutifully recited their names to police – resulting in the men's rapid apprehension!

21. Wimbledon Jack (see page 42). [*The Blue Cross Animal Welfare Society*]
22. Metropolitan Police horses – left to right, Upstart, Regal and Olga (see pages 41 and 42). [*PDSA*]

23. Tipperary Beauty (see page 43).
[*PDSA*]

24. Luise, the German sniffer pig (see
page 47). [*Werner Franke*]

25. Oscar working with handler Rob
Gray in one of Heathrow's freight sheds
(see page 48). [*Chris Lee*]

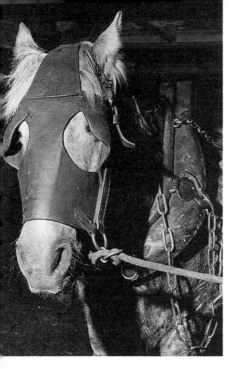

26. Unknown pit pony (see page 49). [*British Coal Corporation*]
27. Pit ponies Andy and Pink coming up from Easington Colliery, Co. Durham, for the last time, with horsekeeper Ernest Robinson (see page 49). [*British Coal Corporation*]
28. A pit canary with miner (see page 51). [*British Coal Corporation*]

29. Barry, on display at the Natural History Museum in Berne (see page 53). [*Berne Natural History Museum*]

30. Police dog Lorna (see page 55). [*RSPCA*]

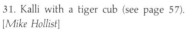

31. Kalli with a tiger cub (see page 57). [*Mike Hollist*]

32. Faith (see page 59). [*PDSA*]

33. Lord Miles with one of 'his' kittens (see page 60). [*Coventry Evening Telegraph*]

34. Lucia and one of 'her' ducklings (see page 60). [*Gillian Davis*]
35. Sidney and the baby hedgehogs (see page 61). [*Phil Callaghan*]
36. Nipper (see page 65). [*Elizabeth Winson, RSPCA*]

37. Statue of Balto (see pages 67 and 68). [*Central Park Conservancy – Sara Cedar Miller*]

38. The worst injured horses that survived the Hyde Park bomb outrage. Sefton is second from the right (see page 72). [*Press Association*]

39. 'America's First Lady of Space' – Miss Baker (see page 75). [*NASA*]

40. Portrait of Tschingel (see page 79). [*Alpine Club Library*]

Chapter Six

A Friend in Need . . .

STORIES OF ANIMALS helping one another come from many sources and at an animal sanctuary in Surrey, some rather unusual friendships have flourished. Few people can fail to be moved by the love and devotion shown by certain animals towards their fellow creatures and in the case of 'fostering', this is not only confined to animals of the same species, as many of the stories illustrate.

At the PRO-Dogs charity annual dinner, where medals for bravery and devotion are presented to nominated dogs, one recipient of a gold medal was Kalli, although her award was not for saving human lives.

Kalli, a good natured dog with a weakness for crisps and chocolate, lived with her owners Stuart and Beatrice Symington who ran the Guilsborough Wildlife Park where Kalli was widely known as 'Super-mum'. Kalli never had puppies of her own but her mothering instincts saved the lives of many other animals. During her lifetime she fostered lion cubs, pumas, foxes, pygmy goats and a leopard. One story tells of a baby badger found unconscious and paralysed in a country lane. It was brought to the Park where Kalli's owners managed to revive it. The four-week-old badger cub, which they named Sophie, was so weak it was feared she would not survive, but with Kalli's tender care and a diet of milk and baby food, Sophie's condition soon started to improve. The dog, a protective and loving 'mother', nursed Sophie back to health and within a few weeks the young badger was fit enough to be released.

Kalli usually slept in the nursery room with whatever animal she was rearing. Every morning when she woke, the black and tan mongrel would walk round the Park enclosures, where-upon the other animals would come running to greet her. She loved nothing better than to play ball and chase the seals up and down the bank of their pool and she was no stranger to television either, appearing on a popular television programme with a leopard cub called Toffi. Kalli died in 1985 and a headstone at the Wildlife Park marks her grave, which many people have visited.

However, that is not the end of Kalli's story for her name now lives on with the formation of the Kalli Animal and Wildlife Sanctuary Trust. The work of the Trust involves caring for lost, abandoned or injured pets and wildlife, and foster homes are found whenever possible. Through its fund-raising efforts and generous donations the Trust is now seeking to realize its ambition of building a sanctuary, so that its valuable work may continue to grow.

The Royal Society for the Prevention of Cruelty to Animals was founded in June 1824 and became the first animal welfare organization in the world. Amongst its founder members was the MP William Wilberforce who had worked to abolish slavery, and in 1840 the Society was granted its 'Royal' prefix by Queen Victoria. In Victorian society the Queen was considered something of a radical because she showed compassion for all animals. This view was emphasized in 1887 when she instructed a medal to be made for use by the RSPCA and returned the original design for amendment because it had not included a cat. The fact that she could be bothered about animals at all was considered amazing – but to regard a cat as important was thought to be quite incredible.

The RSPCA aims to promote kindness and prevent cruelty to all animals, and during the war the Society decided to award inscribed collars to those animals who willingly gave their services. These days, as already mentioned, the Society presents a Plaque for Intelligence and Courage in an attempt to recognize and honour the bravery of animals.

Cats, as well as dogs, have displayed tremendous courage and devotion to those they love and many a cat has put its life in danger rescuing its own family or a companion. One incident from the Second World War, recounted by an RSPCA Inspector, concerned a cat who forgot her own fears in her anxiety to save a canine friend. Her unselfishness undoubtedly saved his life.

The Inspector recalled that on one particular occasion, after searching for hours amongst the rubble, he found this dishevelled cat. After some persuasion she drank a saucer of milk. The Inspector then tried to coax her into a basket, but although she was frightened, she would not leave the ruins and even tried to climb back into the hole through which she had just come. Further digging eventually unearthed a small, badly wounded dog which had been crouching, terrified, in the bomb hole. The dog was lifted out, to the apparent satisfaction of the cat, and it was later discovered that the two animals were the inseparable pets of a family bombed on the night of the raid.

Some people believe that dogs and cats are natural enemies and yet many owners would refute such ideas, saying that their particular pets are the best of friends. Numerous stories of the devotion between family pets were told during the war, when animals endeavoured to help each other in times of trouble.

One dog called Jackie, a brown and white mongrel, always offered his assistance to the family cat during an air raid. The cat had a number of kittens so, one at a time, Jackie would carry them very carefully to the shelter whilst the cat trotted alongside, supervising the proceedings. When the danger was over, however, Jackie promptly retired to his bed – the task of carrying the kittens back, being left solely to the cat!

Another cat's premonition managed to save her kitten's life when their home was bombed during the Second World War. Faith was a homeless tabby and white cat who wandered into the church of St. Augustine in London one day. The rector decided to give her a home and Faith was often seen going in and out of the church, sometimes attending a service, when she would take her place in a pew or choir stall and adopt a quiet, dignified pose.

In the summer of 1940, Faith produced a beautiful black and white kitten called Panda and the two slept upstairs in the vicarage. On Friday 6 September, Faith appeared upset and began pacing the floor, searching every room in the building. Eventually, she took Panda down three flights of stairs and placed the kitten in a recesss in the wall. The rector tried four times to return the kitten to the top floor but each time, Faith brought it back to the recess. Finally the rector relented and Faith's basket was also brought down and the cat settled happily beside her kitten.

Three nights later, whilst the rector was away from home, the vicarage was bombed. The building received a direct hit. The house caught fire and when the rector returned the next morning, only smouldering ruins remained. In desperate hope he called out to Faith and in return heard a faint meow. Amidst the wreckage, the recess still stood firm and the rector was overjoyed to see Faith sitting calmly with her kitten between her paws. Firemen came to the rescue, bringing out the pair, and a few minutes later the floor collapsed completely into the burning rubble. Faith and Panda were moved to a safer part of London and although not eligible for the Dickin award, a special silver medal was engraved as a tribute to Faith's 'steadfast courage' and presented to her by the PDSA.

Faith's picture and certificate were hung in the Tower Chapel as a reminder of her bravery, just as other animals have been honoured for their unfailing love and devotion.

Two kittens who were guests of Lord Miles soon realized they had found a friend willing to cater to their every need. Lord, a large German Shepherd and trained guard dog, provided some tender loving care when his mistress Patricia Miles found the kittens abandoned under a pile of cardboard in Coventry. The kittens thrived on a diet of milk and baby food, nestling into Lord's thick fur to sleep. Lord, for his part, took his duties as foster parent very seriously; washing the pair to keep them clean, carrying them about gently in his mouth and keeping a protective eye on them. The pet guinea pig, called Rosie, also looks for Lord to snuggle up to. In fact Lord, described by people who know him as a sensitive, thoughtful dog, has only one vice – a passion for pickled onions!

Gillian Davis' dog Lucia is another animal with her paws full, as she is a foster-mum to some ducklings, which were hatched in the airing cupboard by her owner. Lucia originally came from an animal sanctuary in Oxford and is so gentle that Gillian was not at all surprised when the dog adopted the young ducks, allowing them to sleep on a bean bag with her. One duckling called Bonnington was found to have a bad hip, so for his exercise Gillian used to take him to the river at Bourton-on-the-Water. There Bonnington could happily paddle along whilst Gillian, Lucia and Baggy (a Bagot goat and Lucia's friend) would all walk alongside, keeping a watchful eye on him.

Another animal at a rescue shelter provided the care needed by two orphaned squirrels. Sophie, a beautiful, all-white stray cat at the RSPCA branch in Cardiff, immediately adopted the two charges whose mother had been shot. Although she had one kitten of her own, Sophie still found time to feed, wash and care for the two babies, thought to be just a few days old. The only thing that seemed to bother her was the fact that they had huge tails, whilst her kitten had a comparatively small one. Also, as the squirrels got older, they liked to hold on to Sophie's tummy with their tiny claws which their adoptive mother found rather uncomfortable, although she put up with it stoically. The squirrels thrived and were soon introduced to baby food, cereal, nuts and fruit, and eventually they became old enough to be released back into a wildlife sanctuary. Meanwhile, both cat and kitten were happily re-homed, and Sophie's days as a foster-mum and newspaper celebrity were over.

A mongrel who looked after four baby hedgehogs helped them to survive and in doing so, saved his own life. Sidney came into the care of the RSPCA animal centre at Bawtry, South Yorkshire, after he was found wandering the streets, abandoned and very frightened. Within a few days, staff at the centre were able to gain his confidence and Sidney showed them just what a friendly dog he could be. However, as dogs are unable to be kennelled indefinitely, time seemed to be running out for the affectionate mongrel. On the very day he was due to be put to sleep, four orphaned hedgehogs were admitted to the centre, cold, hungry and with their eyes still closed. Staff carefully placed them in a cardboard box next to a radiator and almost immediately Sidney came over to investigate. After sniffing the box and viewing its occupants, he lay down beside it and went to sleep.

From then on Sidney took over the welfare of the tiny hedgehogs, allowing them to snuggle up to him and keeping a watchful eye over them when they were feeding. Staff were convinced that the warmth and protection the dog provided for his charges, helped them to survive. Following the publicity which the event attracted, the mongrel was offered a new home with caring owners, so the kindness Sidney gave resulted in his own happy reprieve.

One dog, literally snatched from the grave by his enemy,

was Percy the Chihuahua. Micky, an eight-year-old Jack Russell terrier belonging to Mr and Mrs Perks, saved Percy, even though the two dogs were arch rivals and always snapped at each other whenever Percy's mistress, Christine, visited Micky's home to see her parents.

One day it was discovered that three-year-old Percy had been involved in a road accident, and when the family found his lifeless body with no sign of heartbeat, they assumed he was dead. Percy was buried in a bag in the garden by Christine's father, Bill Perks, but within two hours Micky was pawing at the grave, frantically trying to dig up the little dog. At last he managed to pull the Chihuahua out of the bag and licked Percy in an effort to revive him. Then Micky tried to alert Mr and Mrs Perks by whining and pawing at their legs but they took no notice until Mrs Perks spotted Percy's body lying on the path. Thinking that Micky had been involved in some macabre deed, they scolded their dog. It was not until Mr Perks went to rebury Percy that he realized the truth: Percy was still alive. Bill and his wife quickly wrapped Percy in a towel, then telephoned Christine and her husband who took the Chihuahua to a vet. For a few days Percy's life hung in the balance but it was not long before he was standing up and wagging his tail again, although he was not a bit grateful to Micky.

The little Jack Russell was presented with a Plaque by the RSPCA and a gold medal from PRO-Dogs, although the incident did not mellow either of the dogs; they still enjoyed sparring with each other and remained, as always, the best of enemies.

Canine instincts, besides saving lives, also come in useful in everyday situations. One lady explained how, when walking her Dobermann one day, they had to pass a large sheepdog and its mistress. The Dobermann was a notorious fighter and on spotting the other dog, his hackles rose and every muscle tensed. His owner feared the worst, but as they drew closer the Dobermann suddenly relaxed and, averting his eyes, walked straight past. Mystified, his owner turned to the lady with the sheepdog who revealed softly, 'He's blind'.

Another account illustrates further the rapport and friendship which can exist between dogs. A customer was amused to see a lovely Irish Setter standing outside a butcher's shop one day. As the door opened, the dog trotted up to the counter and caught the large bone that was thrown to him. He wagged his tail in thanks and ran out, only to return minutes later to do exactly the same thing again, making off with another big bone. The customer looked bewildered but the butcher explained that the dog, Rusty, lived with another dog called Red and the two were very fond of each other. Some time ago Red had been hit by a car and was now lame, half blind and unable to move about very much. Every day Rusty would call at the butcher's to collect a bone for Red and then come back for one for himself. The butcher said he had not the heart to refuse such a devoted friend.

Rats may not be a species that immediately springs to mind when thinking of creatures showing compassion for their fellow animals. However, there have been accounts of young rats helping older, blind ones on their travels, and a miner in Wales was astonished by the touching devotion shown by one rat in a particular instance. The miner was apparently feeding a rat with the remains of his lunch when it suddenly ran off into the darkness with a small piece of rope between its teeth. Shortly afterwards, it reappeared to continue the meal accompanied by another rat, evidently blind, hanging on tightly to the other end of the rope.

During the 19th century a clergyman told how he found in his house a brown rat which quickly became quite tame and friendly. One night the man woke with a start after being bitten sharply on the cheek by the rat – but he was even more alarmed to find the drapes surrounding his four-poster bed on fire! The clergyman fled the house which was burnt to the ground, but he never saw his little four-legged saviour again.

Rats have been found to have an adaptable and curious nature and perhaps it was their excellent learning abilities which persuaded the US army to train them to detect land mines. Their success rate was reputed to be 100 per cent. Occasionally they even managed to turn the tables on their human examiners. One rat was placed in an exercise wheel whilst an automatic counter monitored the number of rotations. The rat's progress was checked some time later and the observer was greeted by the sight of the animal reclining on its back outside the contraption whilst it nonchalantly spun the wheel with a forepaw!

The Seal Sanctuary at Gweek in Cornwall cares for seals washed ashore, some suffering from starvation, injuries and pneumonia. Where possible the seals, once fit and well, are returned to the sea but some may be too badly injured to face life in the wild again. A few seals have been adopted by groups or individuals who can then keep a check on their progress, and two seals who became quite an attraction at the Sanctuary were Simon and Sally.

The Sanctuary was first started at St. Agnes in Cornwall and in the early days Simon arrived, aged only about four weeks, emaciated and suffering from lung congestion. Ken Jones who runs the Sanctuary weaned him on sprats and gradually the seal showed signs of improvement. Later, an antibiotic was included in his food by slitting open a mackerel and placing the powder inside. Although Simon had a good appetite and was putting on weight, he still found it difficult to breathe and extra care was taken to make sure he was kept warm.

Visitors to the Seal Sanctuary became interested in Simon; he had recovered well but as his lungs were permanently damaged he could never go back to the sea. To entertain the holiday-makers, one of Simon's favourite tricks was to climb on to the life-belt and move his rear flippers slowly so that he travelled up and down the pool in his own special boat. Another game, this time at the visitors' expense, was to suddenly grab the end of the hose-pipe and squirt water over the unsuspecting audience! Because of his antics, the children were especially fond of Simon, often making a special visit to say goodbye to him at the end of their holidays.

Soon Sally joined Simon in the pool. She had been blinded by oil from the Torrey Canyon disaster. The two seals quickly became firm friends and were, before long, inseparable. Simon, despite his own poor health, was very protective of Sally and rarely strayed far from her side. As visitors increased, posters were displayed giving information about the two youngsters.

As time went on, Ken Jones found that he had more seals than he could cope with, but fortunately he was able to obtain a grant for the completion of a larger sanctuary at Gweek. Many of the seals were moved from St. Agnes to their new home but, unfortunately, it was not to be for Simon and Sally. Simon's health deteriorated and one lung eventually collapsed

– within a short time he was dead. Sally was inconsolable. Her blindness had made her nervous and because of this she had seemed to depend on Simon. He had become her protector and guardian, even comforting her with cuddles only a few hours before his death.

Sally somehow knew that Simon had died, although she still clung to his body with her flippers and when Ken tried to comfort her, she did not resist him. Instead she lay her head on his arm and to Ken's distress, he found that she appeared to be crying. (Seals' eyes water normally but these seemed to be genuine tears.) Just over a week later Sally pined to death and Ken buried the two seals side by side.

One farm dog concerned with the safety of other animals is sheepdog Nipper who lives at Ansty Farm, West Sussex. When he was younger, Nipper always lived outside, sleeping in his kennel near the house, although he now occasionally prefers the comforts of his basket in the kitchen. Described as a very affectionate dog by those who know him, Nipper loves having his tummy rubbed – even though it is usually dirty from lying in the mud. He is also famous for his 'Nipper Lean' – a forceful and endearing lean, emphasized by a nudge of his head on the recipient's leg and accompanied by a wagging tail.

When the lambing season starts, the young ones are sometimes kept in a barn and Nipper's self-appointed task is to keep a protective eye on these charges and not allow them to stray too far. In fact it is sometimes difficult to get him away from the lambs, such is his devotion to 'his' flock. However, it was this dedication that helped to save about 300 ewes and lambs one February night when fire broke out in the barn.

All creatures instinctively fear fire and smoke and it was not long before the terrified cries of the animals brought farm worker Patrick Leaney and his wife Jayne to the scene. Unfortunately, even in a short space of time the smoke had become so dense that it was impossible for them to enter the barn. But they watched in amazement as Nipper repeatedly raced into the building in an attempt to save his sheep.

He worked without commands, suffering burnt paws, toxic fumes and smoke filled lungs, bringing out small batches of ewes and lambs as best he could. Some of the very young lambs refused to be moved and this drove desperate mothers back into the barn even after they had been taken to safety. .

Time and again the brave sheepdog entered the fire and even managed to drive out some cows and calves, trapped at the other end of the building.

Despite suffering considerable pain, Nipper soon recovered from the ordeal and was awarded a 'Devotion to Duty' medal by PRO-Dogs and an RSPCA plaque as a tribute to his courage.

Another courageous dog, Huey, a two-year-old Spaniel cross, has no fear of heights which proved lucky for Bo the Boxer when she plummeted 70 feet over a cliff edge near Bristol. Huey did not hesitate to go to the rescue, picking her way carefully down the cliff face in order to reach Bo and then guiding the dog back up the cliff. When Bo hesitated because of her injuries, Huey pushed her friend the rest of the way. The Boxer was taken for veterinary treatment but was soon feeling fit again, meanwhile Huey received an RSPCA plaque for her courage. The Spaniel's owners think that their dog's sure-footedness arose because of her friendship with cats. Everywhere that cats went, Huey would follow and she would spend ages balancing on the garden fence!

In Surrey, a rest home for donkeys also provides a sanctuary for other creatures such as dogs, cats, goats and horses – some 1,000 animals in all. The owner, Mrs Kay Lockwood, says that a special camaraderie exists between the animals and this has been demonstrated in the past by the blind donkeys who were looked after by the other sighted animals. Whenever a blind donkey decided to go for a walk, he was always accompanied by two sighted ones, positioned on either side, to gently steer him away from obstacles and ensure he did not get into danger.

In other instances when Charlie (a bottle-fed lamb) escaped the grounds and then found himself locked out, the animals all rallied round. Uproar ensued and no one got any peace until Charlie was let back in.

Many of the animals have their own favourite friend, such as the injured fallow deer brought to the home, who now has an inseparable companion in the shape of a goat called Poppy. Another unlikely duo are Domino the goose and his friend, also called Charlie. The pair patrol the grounds and act as excellent 'Watchmen' – Charlie being a huge bull, who has the run of the place at night!

Chapter Seven

Great Achievements

G REAT ACHIEVEMENTS come in many forms –
from marathon treks to recovery from serious
injuries, from space travel to mountaineering. It seems that
wherever man has gone, animals have followed, or in some
cases got there first! Many extraordinary stories make front
page news but one lasting tribute is a race which takes place
each year commemorating the Nome serum run.

In the winter of 1925 a wireless crackled, repeating a
desperate message that was to result in twenty men and over a
hundred dogs crossing the Alaskan wilderness in a race
against time. The journey that those heroes undertook is re-
lived in March every year by competitors in the Iditarod Trail
Race, one of the most famous tests of endurance in the world.

Nome, a former gold rush town in Alaska, was in the grip of
a diphtheria epidemic and as bad weather made flying
impossible, a series of dog sled teams set off to cover the 675
miles carrying the antitoxin serum. Starting on 28 January, the
first team began the journey from Nenana, near Fairbanks,
travelling the old mail route which connected outposts from
Anchorage to Nome.

The darkness of the Arctic winter, with temperatures
dropping to 60°F below zero and driving blizzards, made the
trek even more hazardous for the relay teams; at times
visibility was so bad the drivers could not even see their own
dogs. Teams were headed by such men as 'Wild Bill' Shannon,
Jackscrew (a Koyukuk Indian) and champion 'musher'
Leonhard Seppala. It was Seppala with his dog Togo who led
his team over the frozen but perilous Norton Bay, saving
valuable time.

Gunnar Kaasen and lead dog Balto travelled the final relay
and at one point the dog prevented the entire team from going

into the freezing water of the Topkok River. Further on, gusts of wind, sometimes approaching hurricane force, overturned the sled at Bonanza Flats and the serum fell off, but Kaasen found it again, using his bare hands. At last on the morning of 2 February, Balto led the team into Nome whereupon Kaasen tended first to his dogs, struggling to pull ice splinters out of Balto's bleeding paws.

After touring America with Gunnar Kaasen, Balto and the other dogs ended up in a small Los Angeles dime museum. They were subsequently discovered by George Kimble who was outraged at their fate and mounted a successful campaign for their rescue. In 1927, amidst much celebration, the dogs were brought to Cleveland where they spent the remainder of their days enjoying a well-earned rest. Balto died on 14 March 1933 at the age of eleven and his body was preserved and mounted at The Cleveland Museum of Natural History. A bronze statue of him was placed in Central Park, East Drive at 66th Street, and is New York's only statue commemorating a dog.

The Iditarod Trail is now the location for a race that stretches across mountain ranges, frozen wastes and along the Yukon Valley. In the race, the 'Number One' position is listed but is always left blank. It is reserved for the heroes of the 1925 serum run.

Stories of animals trekking miles – across country that is new to them – in order to reach home or their owners, have been recounted for many years and it still remains a mystery as to exactly how they manage such feats. Of course some animals travel unwittingly; they hide in the boots of cars and it is only by mere chance that after many miles they are discovered. However, a cat called Beatle journeyed some 75 miles during the winter of 1986, suffering intense cold and deep snow, to return to his birthplace.

Beatle was born in Bladbean near Canterbury and besides being a jet black affectionate 'live-wire', he had the disconcerting habit of nipping people on the nose. When only a few months old, he went to live with the Lefever family in North Kensington, London, but his wanderlust took him all over the neighbourhood and he frequently had to be evicted from the basement of the local supermarket. This restlessness increased with the arrival of another cat called Gemima in the

Lefever household, and one day Beatle never returned home.

The family thought they had lost him forever, but in April 1987 he turned up in Bladbean where he enjoyed celebrity status once his story became known.

One of the greatest journeys ever made, was by a cat called Sugar who travelled an incredible 1,500 miles from California to Oklahoma when his owners, Mr and Mrs Woods, moved house. As the cat was terrified of cars, it was agreed he should remain with a neighbour, but Sugar had other ideas and some three weeks after his owners' departure the cat set off on his own marathon journey.

Just over a year later, Mrs Woods was startled when a cat of the same appearance as Sugar, suddenly leapt on to her shoulder when she was in the garden one day. Whilst the animal was an incredible likeness, Mrs Woods refused to believe it could be her beloved pet until she stroked him and found the same deformity of hip joint that Sugar had. A quick telephone call to her former neighbours subsequently confirmed Sugar's disappearance shortly after she and her husband had left for Oklahoma.

It is amazing what many animals will go through rather than face separation from their owners. It would seem that the perils of an unknown journey are preferable to the loss of a beloved master (or several masters) as was the case of a black and tan terrier called Boxer. He was attached to a whole group of soldiers in the South Staffordshire regiment and was constantly at their side both day and night.

When the regiment had to travel by train to Assiut, some 200 miles away, Boxer naturally went along too. The dog positioned himself near an open window but not long after starting the journey, he accidentally fell out. When the soldiers saw him lying on the track apparently lifeless, they presumed he was dead. However, within a few days of their arrival at Assiut, Boxer appeared, thin and limping but otherwise none the worse for his long journey by road. Having had little food on the 200-mile trip, Boxer was weak for a time but with loving care and attention provided by his friends, he was soon his old self again.

Another Terrier called Prince was so devoted to his master, James Brown, that he was inconsolable when the man left for the Front in 1914 with the 1st North Staffordshire regiment.

Prince moped for hours, lying with his head on his paws, then finally one day he left his home in Hammersmith and disappeared. A couple of weeks later he had tracked down his master in a trench at Armentières, after sneaking amongst troops who were crossing the channel. The dog's amazing intuition had enabled him to find James Brown, a feat which many found hard to believe. His appearance caused such a stir that he was made regimental mascot and stayed with his owner until the end of the war.

Bandoola was a famous elephant working in Burma at the time of the Japanese invasion in 1942. He was born in November 1897 and was named after General Maha Bandoola, a great patriot, who fought and died for the independence of his country.

The elephant always enjoyed fun and games and forever seemed to be getting into trouble, like the time he got stuck in a swamp and had to be hauled out by the largest 'tusker'. Bandoola also managed to slip on boulders in the river, walk on burning cinders and poke his trunk into a pot of hot oil. When he was older he was not much better. One day he got loose in a pineapple grove and ate about 900 pineapples, resulting in severe colic, but he recovered, apparently none the worse for the experience.

In 1944 the final evacuation of Burma took place and Bandoola was chosen to lead a party of forty-five elephants, eight calves and 198 people across particularly difficult terrain. High in the mountains they reached the most dangerous spot where steps had been cut in the sandstone rock, just big enough to take an elephant's foot. With his handler Po Toke sitting on his head, Bandoola carefully negotiated the steps, at times looking as though he was standing on his hind legs. Then he continued along a narrow path with a sheer drop on one side. The other elephants, as predicted, all followed Bandoola, and when they halted, the back legs of some of the animals were strained to such an extent that they would not stop quivering. The party eventually reached their destination, a tea plantation, with Bandoola carrying a pannier on his back containing eight sick children all with a high fever and some delirious.

Dolphins have been the subject of myths and legends for centuries and a picture showing a boy on a dolphin is believed to have been painted some 2,000 years ago at Pompeii, near Naples. In modern times, the Americans have trained dolphins to carry messages, tools and even detect mines, but it is the dolphin's affinity with men and their extraordinary perception which makes them so special.

Many people believe that dolphins come to the aid of those in distress in the water and this was certainly true for one boy who found himself in danger off the coast of Australia. Three teenagers were surfing at a bay, north of Sydney, accompanied by a small school of dolphins, when suddenly the dolphins started to get restless. Moments later, one of the boys was attacked and bitten by a shark and as he cried for help, his friends noticed that all the dolphins turned towards the shark's fin. After some intense splashing about, the shark disappeared, much to the boys' relief, and the three teenagers were able to get back to shore. It seemed that the dolphins had come to the boy's rescue by driving the shark away, even though it is their natural enemy. Despite such a formidable opponent, a dolphin can kill a shark by ramming it and with a top speed of around 30 m.p.h. they can make quite an impact!

However, it is the intelligence of dolphins which continues to amaze us and in an instance off the Cornish coast, a dolphin called Donald demonstrated his 'sixth sense'. A group of divers had chartered a boat and were practising life-saving drills when Donald – nicknamed 'Beaky' – decided to join in, appearing to take great delight in disrupting the proceedings. He insisted on playing with the divers, pushing the 'victim' and 'rescuer' apart with his nose, and before long the exercise had to be abandoned.

Later that afternoon the party were diving to a wreck when one of the group got into difficulties. He managed to reach the surface but his life-jacket had punctured and was full of water. The man signalled his distress and started to sink. Immediately the person acting as look-out, dived into the water but was alarmed to see Donald swimming towards the diver. Fearing that the dolphin would think it was another game and push the man away, the rescuer swam with some trepidation. However, his doubts were unfounded as Donald seemed to sense that this was a real drama and instead of playing with the man, the dolphin was gently supporting him from beneath. Even as the diver was being helped back to the boat,

Donald continued his support and even seemed to be towing the man along. As the diver was pulled aboard, the rescuer stood on the diving ladder whilst Donald watched intently with his head out of the water. He did not even attempt to pull at the flippers of the rescuer – a trick he sometimes did when he wanted the person to stay in the water and play longer.

It is known that dolphins make people happy and one lady suffering from cancer, confided her fears to a dolphin before she felt able to face her family. She said that having played with the dolphins she felt able to face the future and even years later, she had no doubt that they had helped her to survive a very traumatic period of her life.

The International Dolphin Watch founded by Dr Horace Dobbs, is a non-profit making organization for the study and conservation of dolphins. One of their recent projects is named Operation Sunflower and aims to investigate whether dolphins can have a beneficial effect on people suffering from clinical depression.

Sefton was a horse who unexpectedly found himself in the limelight and who became a national celebrity following the explosion of a bomb at Hyde Park Corner in July 1982. Sefton was born in Ireland in 1963 and spent the first four years of his life in fields at County Waterford. The majority of the horses chosen for the Household Cavalry are bred in Ireland. Sefton was a rather lively youngster who loved to dance and buck and at first it was doubtful that he would make the grade. The Household Cavalry also has specific colour requirements for its horses: black for the officers' mounts and troop horses, grey for the trumpeters and 'coloureds' for drumhorses. Sefton was black with four white socks and a white blaze on his face, and despite his unruly behaviour it was difficult not to admire his handsome presence.

Initially Sefton failed at the remount pass-out. All the horses have to get used to bands, traffic and waving handkerchiefs, but Sefton kept breaking into a canter and then stopping abruptly, all the time snorting loudly. Sefton was the only one who failed to qualify as a troop horse. Although he was in disgrace as a result of this, Sefton was needed for Trooping the Colour. Unfortunately, on that occasion too, his performance left a lot to be desired and instead of a dignified walk he kept breaking into a trot, as well as shying and dancing in the ranks.

Eventually Sefton managed to qualify at the remount pass-out but later, after unseating a corporal, he was relegated to the training school for recruits. There he was in his element, delighting in throwing off bad or inattentive riders. Sefton then spent several years in Germany where he showed a liking for cross-country competition. In 1974, when he was ten years old, he returned to England. This time he resumed his duties at the Barracks in London with a degree of maturity and performed sedately at the Jubilee Celebrations in 1977 and at the wedding of Prince Charles to Lady Diana Spencer in 1981.

In July 1982 Sefton was among the new guard of the Household Cavalry as they made their way to Whitehall. Just as they approached Hyde Park Corner a bomb, concealed in a nearby car, was detonated, killing some members of the guard and several horses. Sefton, the oldest horse, was the most badly injured of the survivors. A razor-sharp piece of metal had severed his jugular vein and he was so weak that the vet could only give him a fifty-fifty chance of recovery. However, by the evening Sefton was eating a bran mash, and after some twenty-eight pieces of shrapnel had been removed from his body, he slowly began to get better.

The barracks were deluged with cards and messages of goodwill, including ones from the Royal Family, the Pope and the Prime Minister. The stall-holders of Covent Garden sent fruit and vegetables for the horses, whilst members of the public sent in a total of a quarter of a million polo-mints as a 'get-well' treat!

As Sefton continued to improve, a painting of him was auctioned in aid of the Army Benevolent Fund, raising more than £12,000, and 15,000 greeting cards printed from the painting were all sold within three weeks. Horse-lovers and well-wishers flocked to purchase Sefton ashtrays, pendants and medallions, such was the feeling for the horse who had become a national symbol of courage and resilience.

On his return from the Royal Army Veterinary Corps Centre at Melton Mowbray where he had been convalescing, Sefton was able to resume his work and was honoured as 'Horse of the Year' at the annual Horse of the Year Show in London.

Another animal who made front-page news, this time in the Autumn of 1986, was Jambo, a 28-stone, male Silverback gorilla who lives at the Jersey Wildlife Preservation Trust.

Five-year-old Levan Merrit, visiting the Wildlife Park with his family, was placed over the safety barrier and on to the boundary wall of the gorilla enclosure by his father, who then turned away for a moment to pick up another child. Meanwhile, Levan tried to stand up and, losing his balance, fell 12 feet into the enclosure, landing on the concrete water drain at the bottom. Jambo and his family of three wives and their offspring were some 50 yards away at the time, waiting to go indoors for their afternoon meal, but on hearing the commotion from frantic onlookers, they decided to investigate what all the fuss was about. The gorillas were inquisitive and whilst not intentionally wishing to harm the child, there was the possibility that they may have tried to play with him.

However, without showing any signs of aggression, Jambo bent over the boy who was unconscious, sniffed him all over, stroked him gently and discovered that he was bleeding. A female gorilla, Nandi, also appeared curious but Jambo firmly shouldered her out of the way and then placed himself between the rest of his family and the child. He continued to sit quietly, looking up at the crowds to see what was going to happen next.

After a few minutes Levan moved, cried and appeared to look at Jambo. This seemed to upset the huge gorilla who then decided to take his family back to the building, where staff had arranged for their immediate entry. An ambulance crew member amongst the spectators jumped into the enclosure and Levan was lifted out and taken to hospital suffering from head injuries and a broken arm. The child gradually made a satisfactory recovery whilst Jambo received world-wide acclaim for his gentle and concerned reaction.

David Attenborough spoke to the Jersey Wildlife Preservation Trust shortly after the incident and said that having met wild gorillas during the making of the BBC television series *Life On Earth*, he was not at all surprised by Jambo's sensitive reaction. It seems that the way in which animals are managed at the JWPT encourages their natural instincts and relationships to develop. This episode certainly indicated that in this sort of environment the true nature of an animal can be preserved.

Gorillas have been kept in captivity for over a century and it was once believed impossible that they could ever breed in such circumstances. Nevertheless, in 1956 the first birth was recorded and now the JWPT is one of the most successful centres in the world for breeding this threatened animal.

Jambo was born in Basle Zoo in Switzerland on 17 April 1961 and was the first captive-bred infant to be reared by its mother. He is now believed to have sired more offspring than any other gorilla in captivity. All the animal enclosures at the JWPT have been carefully designed to suit the particular needs of the inhabitants, and staff are also well aware of the dietary requirements of the animals in their care. The gorillas, for example, enjoy three main meals a day, interspersed with several forage feeds (consisting mainly of seeds, leaves and pellets) which are scattered around, encouraging the animals to occupy their time in finding them.

The Jersey Wildlife Preservation Trust was founded in 1963 by Gerald Durrell and provides a sanctuary for approximately fifty breeding colonies of endangered species. Situated in a parkland of trees, lakes and gardens, the headquarters at Les Augrès Manor provides an international training centre and scholarship programme to promote conservation breeding units around the world; and as a registered charity the Trust is a non-profit making organization. In conserving animals by captive breeding, the Trust aims to build up stocks whilst actively helping to protect natural habitats, so that in future the creatures can be released back into the wild. As Gerald Durrell himself has said, his greatest ambition is to be able to close the 'zoo's' gates permanently.

'America's First Lady of Space', Miss Baker, achieved fame in May 1959 and weighed in at just a fraction of Jambo's size – a mere one pound. The tiny squirrel monkey became a celebrity as a result of America's space programme, when she was launched into orbit along with a rhesus monkey called Able.

Miss Baker originally came from Peru along with several other monkeys and they all underwent extensive training, designed to determine which one would be a suitable candidate for space travel. Six monkeys were short-listed and undertook a twenty-four hour simulated flight. Notes later stated that Miss Baker had received TLC (tender loving care) from a laboratory technician and the name 'Miss TLC' became her real name, Miss Baker being her 'stage' name.

It was decided that Miss Baker was the most suitable

monkey for the mission and she was taken to Cape Canaveral for the scheduled flight. At last, on 28 May, Able and Baker, dressed in special space suits, were placed in the Jupiter rocket and became the first primates launched by the United States, to survive orbital flight. They reached an altitude of approximately 300 miles at a speed of 10,000 m.p.h. and travelled about 1,500 miles downrange.

Electronic monitors revealed that Miss Baker was mildly startled at lift-off, but when the nose cone of the rocket was recovered later without incident, the two monkeys showed no ill effects from their flight. In fact, Miss Baker promptly ate a banana and a cracker before falling asleep as she was being taken to meet the Press. The little monkey basked in her new-found popularity and seemed to enjoy appearing on national television shows such as *Good Morning, America*. As her fame spread, so many people wanted to visit her that she was moved to the Alabama Space and Rocket Center in Huntsville. There, she enjoyed her retirement in a specially built, climate-controlled home with her friend, another monkey called Big George. She was put on a special diet and given daily vitamins besides receiving a physical check-up once a month, and at the age of twenty-one, she was believed to be the oldest squirrel monkey in captivity.

Two more animals helping to pioneer space travel were Belka and Strelka, who were launched into space by the Russians in 1960. Dogs of a light colour were chosen for the flight in order that the images relayed from Sputnik V should be as clear as possible.

Belka and Strelka were placed inside hermetically sealed cabins which had been equipped with air purifying chemicals and which were maintained at a temperature of between 59°F and 77°F. They were fed a combined food and water, jelly-like mixture from an automatic dispenser and instruments attached to their bodies gave scientists on earth information regarding their blood pressure, temperature, pulse-rate and breathing, as they travelled some 437,000 miles through outer space.

The dogs were not the only passengers on the flight, as rats, mice, flies and plants had also been placed on board. The living cargo spent more than twenty-four hours in space before re-entry was triggered on the 18th orbit and the capsule safely returned. Although they had experienced weightlessness, all the creatures were found to be in good health and back at the base, the dogs showed a preference for some jellied candy whilst the mice tucked into some biscuits. In 1961, Strelka gave birth to a perfectly normal litter of puppies and one of them, Pushinka, was given to America's First Lady, Mrs John F. Kennedy, as a gift from Nikita Khrushchev.

Two American chimpanzees, Enos and Ham, who also experienced space flight, were trained to press levers and to respond to flashing lights by working various switches. A faulty circuit gave Enos some mild electric shocks along with his banana pellet rewards but he continued to perform impeccably and even back on earth, the banana pellets remained a favourite with him. In 1961 Ham's Mercury capsule reached a speed of 5,800 m.p.h. but again a faulty mechanism provided problems as the chimp's oxygen supply ran short and Ham was subjected to a force of 17 g's. However, the chimp performed his tasks very well and was recovered in good condition. He became so well-known that a few years later he was a celebrity attraction at the National Zoological Park in Washington.

Back down to earth again, to a horse and rider who captured the hearts of a nation. The scene was the 1981 Grand National and there was scarcely a dry eye to be seen when the winning horse was led into the enclosure. Racehorse Aldaniti and jockey Bob Champion did something that many thought was impossible. They recovered from serious setbacks; Aldaniti's leg injuries and Champion's cancer, to win the Grand National.

Aldanti was born on a warm June night in 1970 at Harrogate Stud in Yorkshire and named after the owner's four grandchildren, the first two letters being taken from each of the names: Alastair, David, Nicola and Timothy. Aldaniti was sold in 1974 at the Ascot Bloodstock Sales and was later purchased by Nick Embiricos, living in Sussex. The horse excelled at jumping and under trainer Josh Gifford, was prepared for the biggest race of his life. However, Aldaniti's career was plagued by leg troubles and at one point he had to spend seven months confined to his stable, his legs bandaged and painful. In 1979 a severe tendon problem made it look as if he would never race again, but as in the past, Aldaniti put up with the various treatments without complaining and his calm manner and pleasant personality made him a pleasure to handle.

Whilst Aldaniti's career looked in doubt, Bob Champion too, wondered if he'd ever race again when it was discovered he had cancer. However, during Bob's treatment it was Aldaniti who gave him the will to live; it became Bob's dream to ride the horse in the National. The pair suddenly found themselves to be recovered at about the same time and training for the race began in earnest. Their problems were not quite over though, as Aldaniti was almost hit by a speeding car in a narrow lane just one week before the Aintree race. Then, only 72 hours before the horse was due to start his journey to Liverpool, it was announced that the area might have to be sealed off for any movement of livestock, due to a suspected outbreak of foot and mouth disease.

Eventually both Aldaniti and Bob Champion made it to the course and as soon as the race started, Aldaniti wanted to take the lead. In a field of thirty-nine runners, Bob found his horse jumping superbly and although it looked as if John Thorne on Spartan Missile might just make it, the other horse was simply too tired, and Aldaniti won by four lengths. Bob Champion and Aldaniti were led by a jubilant Nick Embiricos to the winner's enclosure where, despite just having run four and a half miles and jumped thirty fences, Aldaniti appeared in fine form, thoroughly enjoying all the attention.

When the party arrived back at Findon, they found that more than 3,000 well-wishers had come to greet them and there were flags, cards and telegrams round the stable door. Aldaniti was in great demand and began attending fund-raising events like a seasoned campaigner. On one occasion, he was taken to Ascot for a parade with Red Rum and Rubstic but Aldaniti thought he was going racing again. When he was finally led back to his box, he was so disgusted that he just stood with his head in a corner and refused to acknowledge anyone.

Nick Embiricos decided to retire Aldaniti and at about that time, discussions were taking place for a film called *Champions* based on Bob's book. Aldaniti himself was used in certain scenes but was also given six 'doubles' – more than some human film stars! However, the horse was a natural performer and seemed to enjoy playing to the camera. Once the filming was over, Aldaniti resumed his fund-raising activities and both horse and jockey were an inspiration to many people. After all, they had fought back against seemingly insurmountable odds to win the National and in doing so became symbols of hope and victory over suffering.

Cliffs seem to have a special lure for dogs, and one named Sampson, a Golden Retriever, who became trapped on a ledge, only survived because of his own ingenuity – and stormy weather! Sampson fell 100 feet at Budleigh Salterton in Devon, dislocating both front paws. He managed to crawl on to a ledge overlooking the English Channel, where he spent days awaiting rescue, huddled against the cold, wet weather. It was lucky for Sampson however, that the weather was so bad as he survived by licking rain water off his coat; had it been sunny, he might not have lived. His owners and volunteers did not give up searching and eventually, after twelve days, he was spotted and lowered to safety.

In the 19th century, people were only just starting to become aware of the needs of animals and there existed many prejudices and ideas which we would find strange today. In mountaineering circles it was common for climbers to take their dogs along, and one animal who scaled the alpine heights was Tschingel, described by some as looking like a large Beagle with her silky brown and white coat. She was born in 1865 in a beautiful Swiss village and was named after the first glacier pass that she crossed.

Tschingel was given to climber Rev W.A.B. Coolidge by his guide, and made many ascents with the rather eccentric man and his Aunt 'Meta'. At times the dog's feet became so sore that Coolidge had some small boots made for her, but she flatly refused to wear them, tearing them off as quickly as he put them on.

Tschingel had two collars; one for everyday wear and one for 'best' which carried silver medallions engraved with the names of the peaks she had climbed. Taking a dog on to the mountains did not seem to hinder the climbers at all and in fact Tschingel, on at least one occasion, guided the party across treacherous glaciers, finding the safest route to avoid the deep, hidden cracks under the snow. In another incident, she was even able to lead an experienced local guide down a stretch of difficult terrain.

She made hundreds of small climbs and approximately sixty-six outstanding ones – in July 1875 climbing all the way to the top of Mont Blanc. After conquering the mountain, Tschingel returned to the village, a heroine. A reception was held in the hotel to celebrate the success and Tschingel 'held court', reclining on a sofa in the drawing room and being visited by numerous admirers. A cannon was even fired at Chamonix in her honour.

She was subsequently made an 'Honorary Member of the Alpine Club' and became the first lady to be admitted to the exclusive circle. As she grew older, she spent more time at home and eventually she died peacefully in her sleep, lying in front of the kitchen fire. She was laid to rest in the garden and a rock, brought specially from the Alps, was later placed as a headstone.

Animal heroes sometimes have their exploits recorded for posterity, but there are countless creatures who go unnoticed as they live and die through our inadequacies, ineptitude and conflicts. It is our good fortune to share our lives with animals and the inscription on a monument at Port Elizabeth in South Africa, seems a fitting tribute to them all:

> The greatness of a nation consists not so much in the number of its people or the extent of its territory as in the extent and justice of its compassion.
>
> *Erected by public subscription in recognition of the services of the gallant animals which perished in the Anglo Boer War 1899–1902.*

USEFUL ADDRESSES

For those charities which collect used postage stamps:–
a) *tear off part of the envelope bearing the postmark – as well as the stamp itself;*
b) *ensure that when cut or torn from envelopes, the perforations are kept intact.*

The American Humane Association
9725 East Hempden Avenue
Denver
Colorado 80231
U.S.A

For further details of membership and how you can support their work, send a self-addressed envelope with return postage to:–
P.O. Box 1266
Denver
Colorado 80201
U.S.A.

The Blue Cross (Incorporating Our Dumb Friends' League)
Animals Hospital
1 Hugh Street
Victoria
London SW1V 1QQ

Tel: (01) 834 4224
     (01) 834 5556

Dogs for the Disabled
Brook House
1 Lower Ladyes Hills
Kenilworth
Warwickshire CV8 2GN

Tel: (0926) 59726
Collects used postage stamps

The Dogs' Home Battersea
4 Battersea Park Road
London SW8 4AA

Tel: (01) 622 3626

The Guide Dogs for the Blind Association
Alexandra House
9 Park Street
Windsor
Berkshire SL4 1JR

Tel: (0753) 855711
Collects used foil/silver paper also used postage stamps

Gweek Seal Sanctuary
Gweek
Nr Helston
Cornwall

Tel: (0326) 22361
Accepts donations of old towels (which are used for drying off the seals)

Hearing Dogs for the Deaf
Training Centre
Little Close
Lower Icknield Way
Lewknor
Oxford OX9 5RY

Tel: (0844) 53898
Collects Green Shield stamps

Helping Hands
Simian Aides For the Disabled,
Inc.
1505 Commonwealth Avenue
Boston
Massachusetts 02135
U.S.A.

Tel: (617) 787 4419

Hill and Knowlton, Inc.
One Illinois Center
111 East Wacker Drive
Chicago
Illinois 60601
U.S.A.

Present the Ken-L Ration Dog Hero
of the Year award

Home of Rest for Old and Sick
Donkeys
Contact: Mrs Kay Lockwood
Farm Cottage
Sandhills
Wormley
Nr Godalming
Surrey GU8 5UX

Tel: (042 879) 2409
Collects Green Shield and Co-Op
stamps

International Dolphin Watch
Parklands
North Ferriby
Humberside HU14 3ET

Tel: (0482) 634895
Collects any information/news about
dolphins

The Jersey Wildlife Preserva-
tion Trust
Les Augrès Manor
Trinity
Jersey
Channel Islands

Tel: (0534) 61949
Collects used postage stamps

Kalli Animal and Wildlife
Sanctuary Trust
Enquiries to: Mr Radford
Pant Glas
Nether Lane
Flore
Northampton NN7 4LR

Tel: (0327) 42000

National Canine Defence
League
1 Pratt Mews
London NW1 0AD

Tel: (01) 388 0137
Collects used postage stamps,
foreign coins and out of mint coins

The People's Dispensary for
Sick Animals
Unit 6B
Ketley Business Park
Telford
Shropshire TF1 4JD

Tel: (0952) 222322
Collects used postage stamps

PRO-Dogs National Charity
Rocky Bank
4 New Road
Ditton
Maidstone
Kent ME20 6AD

Tel: (0732) 848499
Collects used postage stamps

The Royal Air Force Police and Dogs
The Dog Training Centre
RAF Newton
Nottingham

Anyone wishing to donate a dog
should contact:
The Officer Commanding
Dog Support Centre
Royal Air Force
Newton
Nottingham NG13 8HL
or telephone (0949) 20771
extension 330

Royal Society For the Prevention of Cruelty to Animals
Causeway
Horsham
West Sussex RH12 1HG

Tel: (0403) 64181
*Collects used postage stamps
(should be sent to the Fund-raising
Department)*

St. Bernhardiner-Zucht
Hospice du St. Grand-Bernard
CH-1931 Bourg-St-Pierre
Switzerland

Search And Rescue Dog Association
c/o Alison Graham
Gwynne Hart and Assocs
4 Bedford Square
London WC1B 3RA

The Seeing Eye, Inc.
P.O. Box 375
Morristown
New Jersey 07960
U.S.A.

Tel: (201) 539 4425

Bibliography

Brown, Anthony, *Who Cares for Animals – 150 years of the RSPCA*, (William Heinemann, 1974)

Clark, Ronald William, *An Eccentric in the Alps – the Story of W. A. B. Coolidge, the Great Victorian Mountaineer*, (Museum Press Ltd, 1959)

Cooper, Jilly, *Animals in War*, (William Heinemann, 1983)

Cottesloe, Gloria, *The Story of the Battersea Dogs' Home*, (David & Charles, 1979)

Delderfield, Eric R., *Eric Delderfield's Book of True Animal Stories*, (David & Charles, 1970)

Dobbs, Dr. Horace, *Follow a Wild Dolphin*, (Souvenir Press, 1977, Fontana Paperbacks, 1979)

Dobbs, Dr. Horace, *Save the Dolphins*, (Souvenir Press, 1981)

Edwards, Major T.J., M.B.E., F.R.Hist.S., *Mascots and Pets of the Services*, (Gale & Polden Ltd, 1953)

Halstock, Max, *Rats – The Story of a Dog Soldier*, (Victor Gollancz Ltd, 1981)

Jones, Ken, *Seal Doctor*, (Fontana Paperbacks, 1978)

Locke, Angela, *Search Dog*, (Souvenir Press, 1987)

Moss, Arthur W. & Kirby, Elizabeth, *Animals Were There – RSPCA during the War 1939–1945*, (Hutchinson & Co., 1947)

Porter, Valerie, *The Guinness Book of Almost Everything You Didn't Need to Know About Dogs*, (Guinness Superlatives Ltd, 1986)

Richardson, Anthony, *One Man And His Dog – a true story of Antis* (George G. Harrap & Co, 1960)

St. Hill Bourne, Dorothea, *They Also Serve – a History of the PDSA* (Winchester Publications Ltd, 1947)

Sisson, Terence, *Just Nuisance AB – His Full Story* (W. J. Flesch & Partners (PTY) Ltd, 1985)

Squires, Eric, *Pit Pony Heroes*, (David & Charles, 1974)

Tremain, Ruthven, *Animal's Who's Who*, (Routledge & Kegan Paul, 1982)

Tresilian, Liz, *Aldaniti – the story of a champion*, (Victor Gollancz, 1984)

Varley, E., edited by James, Wendy, *The Judy Story – the dog with six lives*, (Souvenir Press Ltd, 1973)

Watson, J. N. P., *Sefton – The Story of a Cavalry Horse* (Souvenir Press Ltd, 1983)

Whitfield, June, *Dog's Tales*, (Robson Books, 1987)

Williams, J. H., *Bandoola*, (Rupert Hart-Davis Ltd, 1953, The New Windmill Series Heinemann Educational Books Ltd, 1962)

Williams, J. H., *Elephant Bill* (Rupert Hart-Davis Ltd, 1965)

Wood, Gerald L., *Guinness Book of Pet Records*, (Guinness Superlatives Ltd, 1984)

Index